Praise for
Challenging Learning Through Dialogue
by James Nottingham, Jill Nottingham and Martin Renton

James Nottingham's work on Challenging Learning is a critical element of creating Visible Learners. This new series will help teachers hone the necessary pedagogical skills of dialogue, feedback, questioning and mindset. There's no better resource to encourage all learners to know and maximize their impact!

—John Hattie
Professor and Director
Melbourne Education Research Institute
University of Melbourne, Australia

James Nottingham has masterfully explained what dialogue is and how to use it in the classroom through powerful strategies. These powerful strategies challenge students to engage in deep thinking and understanding. The myriad of examples bring the strategies to life, and I could envision the possible student exchanges with the use of these strategies as I was reading.

—Tracy Shiel
Corwin Author/Consultant
Walla Walla, WA

This book is a great tool for educators interested in making dialogue work in the classroom. [It] is really clear and easy to follow, with sample dialogue structures that teachers can use and examples to follow. I recommend it for individual educators, teams [and] districts.

—Kara Vandas
Corwin Author/Consultant
Castle Rock, CO

Sitting among eager students engaged in what James Nottingham calls "exploratory talk" is, indeed, a thrilling experience, because we are witnessing authentic wonder, inquiry, critical thinking and reflection all in pursuit of deeper understanding of complex issues and ideas. In this book Nottingham presents viable approaches for such talk, for learning how to think. One result is "to make us wobble," not in commitment but in considering the thoroughness of all our thinking. This is a splendid contribution to our literature in these days where the matter of rigorous, performance standards is in much need of debate and dialogue.

—John Barell, *Author*
Why Are School Buses Always Yellow? and Problem-Based Learning
New York, NY

Like either side of a coin, language and thinking are inseparably entwined. Our thoughts direct our language and our language conveys our thoughts. Efficacious thinkers, therefore, enhance their thinking by enriching their linguistic capacities. And that is what this valuable book is about. It is a must for teachers and families who wish to have their children learn to think and communicate with greater precision and clarity. Filled with rich background information, myriad protocols, practical learning strategies and vivid examples, this book can teach us all how to listen more attentively and to communicate more thoughtfully. It is what the world needs now.

—Arthur L. Costa, EdD
Professor Emeritus, California State University Sacramento, and
Co-Director, International Institute for Habits of Mind

We know that teachers do too much of the talking in the classroom, and they know it too. But too often their first question is "How do we get students to talk more?" Nottingham, Nottingham and Renton have helped answer that question. *Challenging Learning* is filled with practical advice and important activities that will help increase dialogue in classrooms!

—Peter DeWitt
Author/Consultant
Albany, NY

This work from Nottingham, Nottingham and Renton clearly demonstrates first how to create both the moral and instructional imperative to increase student voice and dialogue for meaning-making between teacher and student in all classrooms. They then articulate countless ways for how to do so in practical, meaningful and relevant ways that allow any teacher to begin to do so tomorrow. This work should be in the hands of every teacher and administrator before they walk into your school.

—Dave Nagel
Author/Consultant
Corwin/NZJ Learning

In my position as the gifted specialist, I work with both students and teachers. I help support teachers in planning to meet the needs of my students as well as working with beginning teachers. All would benefit from incorporating *Dialogue* in [their] content areas. This book could quite frankly change a lot of classroom practices; it wasn't preachy—it was informative and a great guide to engage students.

—Susan Leeds
Gifted Specialist
Winter Park High
Winter Park, FL

James Nottingham thinks most teachers do too much of the talking in the classroom. His newest offering from the Challenging Learning series is a stand-alone exploration of how to use reasonable, student-generated dialogue to move from surface-level learning to deep understanding. Nottingham uses relevant research, instructive examples and a wealth of resource tools to help educators guide students in how to think rather than what to think. Regardless of grade level or discipline, teachers who want to hone their mastery skills will appreciate this useful book.

—Debbie Silver, EdD
Author of Fall Down 7 Times, Get Up 8: Teaching Kids to Succeed
and Deliberate Optimism: Reclaiming the Joy in Education

If we want students to be engaged, active and deep-thinking, we can all learn from the authors of *Challenging Learning Through Dialogue*. This book makes a strong argument for not just allowing students to talk, but for creating communities of trust where students learn how to dialogue with one another in whole-group and small-group settings across the content areas. The authors share sample transcripts, clear charts and helpful lesson ideas for purposefully teaching students how to dialogue. Underpinning all of the examples and lessons is the principle that authentic inquiry and reflective thinking are essentials in our classrooms and our world. After reading this book you will feel inspired and ready to focus on saying less as teachers so your students can say, and therefore learn, more.

—Gravity Goldberg, *Literacy Consultant and Author*
Mindsets and Moves: Strategies That Help Readers Take Charge, Grades 1–8
New York, NY

The best kinds of teaching books do three things: show me what I'm doing, cast a compelling vision for how I could be doing it better, and provide me practical tools for turning the present reality into the compelling vision. With those criteria, I can only call this a new member of the best kinds of teaching books. I am eager to infuse dialogue into the speaking and listening work my students and I do together.

—Dave Stuart, Jr., *Speaker and Literacy Consultant*
Author, A Non-Freaked Out Guide to Teaching the Common Core
Cedar Springs, MI

This book reminds teachers of the power of dialogue to develop deeper learning. It provides a groundbreaking framework with specific strategies teachers can use as they move students toward deeper understanding through dialogue.

—John Spencer
Assistant Professor of Instructional Technology, George Fox University
Author, Confident Voices: Digital Tools for Language Acquisition
Portland, OR

Challenging Learning Through Dialogue provides educators with meaningful, purposeful and practical strategies to create high-quality dialogue. Underpinned by extensive educational research, these methods will help students achieve deep-level thinking and learning through the power of our language. It is inspiring, insightful and a *must*-read for all educators. Absolutely brilliant!

—Sophie Murphy
Clinical Teaching Specialist, Lecturer and Researcher
Science of Learning Research Centre
Melbourne Graduate School of Education, Australia

CHALLENGING
LEARNING Through
DIALOGUE

Challenging Learning Series

The Learning Challenge: How to Guide Your Students Through the Learning Pit

by James Nottingham

Challenging Learning Through Dialogue

by James Nottingham, Jill Nottingham and Martin Renton

Challenging Learning Through Feedback

by James Nottingham and Jill Nottingham

Challenging Learning Through Mindset

by James Nottingham and Bosse Larsson

Challenging Learning Through Questioning

by James Nottingham and Martin Renton

Learning Challenge Lessons, Elementary

by James Nottingham, Jill Nottingham, Lucy Thompson and Mark Bollom

Learning Challenge Lessons, Secondary ELA

by James Nottingham, Jill Nottingham, Lucy Thompson and Mark Bollom

Learning Challenge Lessons, Secondary Mathematics

by James Nottingham, Jill Nottingham, Lucy Thompson and Mark Bollom

Learning Challenge Lessons, Secondary Science/STEM

by James Nottingham, Jill Nottingham, Lucy Thompson and Mark Bollom

James Nottingham ■ Jill Nottingham ■ Martin Renton
Foreword by Douglas Fisher

CHALLENGING LEARNING Through DIALOGUE

Strategies to Engage Your Students and
Develop Their Language of Learning

CORWIN
A SAGE Publishing Company

FOR INFORMATION

Corwin
A SAGE Company
2455 Teller Road
Thousand Oaks, California 91320
(800) 233-9936
www.corwin.com

SAGE Publications Ltd.
1 Oliver's Yard
55 City Road
London, EC1Y 1SP
United Kingdom

SAGE Publications India Pvt. Ltd.
B 1/I 1 Mohan Cooperative Industrial Area
Mathura Road, New Delhi 110 044
India

SAGE Publications Asia-Pacific Pte. Ltd.
3 Church Street
#10-04 Samsung Hub
Singapore 049483

Acquisitions Editor: Ariel Bartlett
Senior Associate Editor: Desirée A. Bartlett
Editorial Assistant: Kaitlyn Irwin
Production Editors: Cassandra Margaret Seibel
 and Melanie Birdsall
Copy Editor: Sarah J. Duffy
Typesetter: Hurix Systems Pvt. Ltd.
Proofreader: Caryne Brown
Indexer: Jean Casalegno
Cover Designer: Janet Kiesel
Marketing Manager: Jill Margulies

Library of Congress Cataloging-in-Publication Data

Names: Nottingham, James, author. | Nottingham, Jill, author. | Renton, Martin, author.

Title: Challenging learning through dialogue : strategies to engage your students and develop their language of learning / by James Nottingham, Jill Nottingham and Martin Renton.

Description: Thousand Oaks, California : Corwin, a SAGE company, [2017] | Series: Challenging learning series | Includes bibliographical references and index.

Identifiers: LCCN 2016044633 | ISBN 9781506376523 (pbk. : alk. paper)

Subjects: LCSH: Questioning. | Communication in education. | Teacher-student relationships.

Classification: LCC LB1027.44 .N67 2017 | DDC 371.102—dc23 LC record available at https://lccn.loc.gov/2016044633

US Edition

This book is printed on acid-free paper.

SFI Certified Sourcing
www.sfiprogram.org
SFI-00453

17 18 19 20 21 10 9 8 7 6 5 4 3 2 1

CONTENTS

Chapter 3: Dialogue to Engage Students   27

Chapter 4: One Way to Learn *How* to Think: Develop Reasoning   35

Chapter 5: Dialogue Groupings   49

Chapter 6: Dialogue Detectives   61

Chapter 7: Dialogue Structures   67

Chapter 8: Mysteries   79

Chapter 9: Odd One Out   107

Chapter 10: Fortune Lines   125

Chapter 11: Philosophy for Children (P4C)   137

Chapter 12: Dialogue Exercises in P4C   151

Appendix 1: Dialogue Detectives   157

Appendix 2: Louis Pasteur Script   158

Repertoire and Judgment Notes   166

References   178

Index   180

LIST OF FIGURES

THE CHALLENGING LEARNING STORY

Challenging Learning was the title I used for my first book back in 2010. I chose the title because it brought together two key themes of my work and it gave a relevant double meaning—challenging the way in which learning takes place and showing how to make learning more challenging.

More recently, Challenging Learning is the name I've given to a group of organizations set up across seven countries. These educational companies bring together some of the very best teachers and leaders I know. Together we transform the most up-to-date and impressive research into best pedagogical practices for schools, preschools and colleges.

This book continues in the same tradition: challenging learning and making learning more challenging. The main difference between this book and the original *Challenging Learning* title is that this one focuses on practical resources for use by teachers, support staff and leaders. There is still some theory, but now the emphasis is on pedagogical tools and strategies. Across this new series you will find books about questions and the zone of proximal development, feedback and progress, mindset and self-efficacy, coaching for professional development, and leadership and organization.

This particular volume focuses on using dialogue to deepen understanding. Here my co-authors and I share some of the best ways to use dialogue to help your students move from a state of "knowing" to a state of "understanding." This includes making connections between concepts and knowledge, ideas and questions, and links between what has been learned before and what is being learned now.

I am delighted to say I have written this book in collaboration with some of my closest colleagues: Martin Renton, Jill Nottingham and our team at Challenging Learning. Together we have blended the best of what we have all been working on for the last twenty years or more.

For the sake of clarity, the term "we" is used to represent ideas from Jill, Martin and me. Individual stories are prefaced with our first names. Where an idea or strategy comes from one of the other authors, we preface that section with their full names, for example, Steve Williams or Richard Kielty.

As you read this book, you will notice that we refer mainly to *teachers* and *teaching*. Please do not take this to mean this book is only for teachers. In fact, the book is aimed at support staff and leaders as much as at teachers. We simply use the terms *teachers* and *teaching* as shorthand for the position and pedagogy of all the professions working in schools.

Most chapters begin with a preview. This is to give you a chance to think about your current practice before diving in to see what our recommendations are. Chatting with a colleague about what you think works well (and how you know it does); what you would like to change; and, in an ideal world, what you would like your pedagogy to be like will definitely help you use this book as the reflective journal it is intended to be.

At the end of each chapter, we include a review. This is focused on repertoire and judgment. A broad repertoire—or tool kit of teaching strategies as some authors call it— is crucial to improving pedagogy. Yet repertoire alone is not sufficient; good judgment is also needed. So, whereas the strategies in this book should be sufficient to broaden your repertoire, your good judgment will come from reflections on your own experiences, from trying out the new strategies with your students and from dialogue with your colleagues. Our suggestions for review are there to help you with your reflections.

Finally, the Next Steps section of each chapter is included to emphasize how much your actions count. As a teacher, teaching assistant or leader, you are among the most powerful influences on student learning. Back when you were a student at secondary school and went from teacher to teacher, you knew exactly which member of staff had high expectations and which had low, which had a good sense of humor and which you suspected had not laughed since childhood. It is the same today. Your students know what your expectations and ethos are. So it is not the government, students' parents or the curriculum that sets the culture (though they all have influence). It is you who sets the culture, and so it is your actions that count most.

With this book I hope we can inspire you to ever more expert actions.

With best wishes,

James Nottingham

FOREWORD

I cannot even count the number of times a student has said to me, "I didn't know what I thought until we talked about it." Dialogue and discussion matter because they help clarify perspectives. They help us understand our own thinking. When engaged in a discussion with other people, we find that our own thinking often becomes clearer. We might have a general idea of our perspective, which is honed and sharpened as we interact with other people. You see, discussing something encourages thinking about that something. And that's what we want in our classrooms: thinking.

When students sit quietly listening to their teacher, we have no idea *if* they are thinking. We also don't know *what* they're thinking. And this is an important point. Students who engage in teacher-pleasing behaviors—looking at the teacher, sitting up in their chairs, being quiet—may not be thinking about the lesson at all. They appear engaged, but may not be learning. I think that there is a big difference between behavioral engagement and cognitive engagement. Unfortunately, too many people (especially administrators) pay attention to behavioral engagement because it's easier to observe.

What makes it easier to tell if students are cognitively engaged is discussion and dialogue. As students interact with each other and their teachers, thinking becomes obvious. It becomes public and available for others to respond to. It becomes fodder for future lessons and interactions that continue to shape students understanding of the world. In other words, discussion and dialogue provide students and their teachers with evidence of learning. There are, of course, other ways to determine if students are learning. But dialogue allows understanding to be modified along the way.

Importantly, it's not just my personal experience that supports the value of discussion and dialogue in the classroom. In John Hattie's (2009) seminal review of educational research, he noted that classroom discussion had an effect size of 0.82. That means that this one thing has the potential to double the speed of learning. When students are engaged in dialogue and discussion, using academic language and their argumentation skills, they are much more likely to accelerate their learning. The hard part is getting discussion to happen in class. When I asked colleagues about what it took for discussion to take hold in the classroom, I received a lot of really good ideas. Here are some of the aspects that have to be in place for classrooms to be places where students feel comfortable to engage in dialogue with their peers:

- Enough background knowledge to have something to say

- Language support to know how to say it

- Topic of interest and an understanding of the task

- An authentic reason to interact

- Expectation of, and accountability for, interactions

- Established community of learners who encourage and support each other

That's where *Challenging Learning Through Dialogue* comes in. This book is filled with specific ideas to facilitate classroom discussion. The authors provide concrete strategies for all of us to use to create learning environments filled with purposeful talk. The chapters include information about establishing a community of learners and supporting academic language development. They provide specific instructional routines that encourage student-to-student interactions. The ideas that they share are concrete and yet adaptable to a variety of classrooms.

Armed with the information in this book, teachers can transform their classrooms and worry less about off-task behavior and wandering minds. When the ideas in this book are implemented, classrooms become places where challenge is accepted because students know that they can rise to those challenges with the support of their peers and their teacher. The authors provide a glimpse into classrooms of the future where students have greater responsibility for their own learning and seek feedback from peers about their learning, all through the dialogue that happens in the classroom. I can't help but think about the impact this could have on the world. Imagine a society in which people engage in authentic interactions, discussions and dialogue with one another, seeking to identify points of agreement, providing evidence for their ideas, reaching consensus and agreeing to disagree. That's a society I'd like to be part of, and I accept my responsibility to contribute to that vision. Do you? If so, the information in this book will help create such a place.

—Douglas Fisher
Professor, San Diego State University
Author, Rigorous Reading *and* Visible Learning for Literacy

ACKNOWLEDGMENTS

Corwin gratefully acknowledges the following reviewers for their editorial insight and guidance:

Peter DeWitt
Author/Consultant
Albany, NY

Susan Leeds
Gifted Specialist
Winter Park High
Winter Park, FL

Dave Nagel
Author/Consultant
Corwin/NZJ Learning
Zionsville, IN

Kara Vandas
Corwin Author/Consultant
Castle Rock, CO

Craig Yen
Fourth-Grade Teacher
Valle Verde Elementary
Walnut Creek, CA

ABOUT THE AUTHORS

James Nottingham is the founder of Challenging Learning, a company based in the United Kingdom, Australia and Scandinavia. His passion is in transforming the most up-to-date research into strategies that really work in the classroom. He has been described by the Swedish Teaching Union as "one of the most talked-about names in the world of school development."

Before training to be a teacher, James worked on a pig farm, in the chemical industry, for the American Red Cross and as a sports coach in a school for deaf children. At university, he gained a first-class honors degree in education. He then worked as a teacher and leader in primary and secondary schools in the United Kingdom before co-founding an award-winning, multimillion-pound social regeneration project supporting schools and businesses across the United Kingdom.

In 2009, James was listed among the Future 500—a "definitive list of the UK's most forward-thinking and brightest innovators."

Jill Nottingham's background is in teaching, leadership and consultancy. She has been a teacher and leader in kindergartens and schools in some of the more socially deprived areas of North East England. During that time, she developed many approaches to teaching children how to learn that are still being used in schools and taught in universities today.

Jill has also trained with Edward de Bono at the University of Malta and has studied for a master's degree in education with the University of Newcastle.

Jill now leads Challenging Learning's preschool and primary school consultancy. She has written many of the Challenging Learning teaching materials, has edited the others and is currently writing three books for schools and two books for preschools. In among this she finds time to be the mother of three gorgeous children!

Martin Renton is the managing director of Challenging Learning, responsible for the outstanding delivery of all long-term development projects. He is also a highly sought-after keynote speaker, leader, facilitator and coach.

Martin's knowledge of pedagogy and leadership is borne out in his experiences in schools and colleges as a teacher, leader, consultant and coach. While he is Challenging Learning's post-16 specialist, his early years' experiences as a nanny (two- to nine-year-olds) then as a teacher and leader in middle schools (nine- to thirteen-year-olds), secondary schools (eleven- to eighteen-year-olds) and colleges (sixteen and older) have given him unique insight into how people learn from the age of two to adulthood. Martin uses these insights to challenge, inspire and engage his audiences.

With a master's degree in educational research from Newcastle University, Martin designs and leads all of Challenging Learning's evaluation processes. He is also trained in the historic craft of drystone-walling and still labors under the impression that he can play the guitar!

CONTRIBUTORS

James Nottingham, Jill Nottingham and Martin Renton have written this book with contributions from the following:

- Mark Bollom
- Louise Brown
- Andy Craig
- Jill Harland
- Dan Henderson
- Richard Kielty
- Bosse Larsson
- Joanne Nugent
- Åse Ranfelt
- Katherine Renton
- Helen Richards
- Phil Thompson
- Steve Williams (author of Chapter 4)

All authors and contributors can be contacted through www.challenginglearning.com.

"The most important attitude that can be formed is that of desire to go on learning."

(Dewey, 1916/2011)

INTRODUCTION

This book has been strongly influenced by the work of John Dewey (1859–1952) and Matthew Lipman (1922–2010). That's not to say we knew either of them! But it is to say the ideas recommended in this book owe much to the Philosophy for Children (P4C) training we took part in early in our careers.

As described in Chapter 11, Matthew Lipman designed the Philosophy for Children process based on the belief that children can and should be encouraged to philosophize. Among his influences were the writings of John Dewey, the American pragmatist who made seminal contributions to pedagogy, philosophy of science, ethics and social theory. Belonging to the tradition of reflective education, both Dewey and Lipman placed thinking and dialogue at the core of educational aims and practices. Furthermore, both writers understood thinking as a process of inquiry. As you read through this book, you will notice that we emphasize these same points—that thinking, dialogue and inquiry should be placed right at the heart of education.

It would be fair to say that our theoretical basis also owes much to the work of the educational psychologist Lev Vygotsky (1896–1934). Among the many ideas he shared with the world, Vygotsky wrote that the communication processes used between people becomes internalized into verbal thought. That is to say that the ideas and processes a person experiences in dialogue with others influence the way in which he or she thinks in the future. Thus external dialogue becomes internal dialogue.

> Every feature in the child's cultural development appears twice: first on the social level, and later on the individual level: first *between* people (*inter*-psychological) and then inside the child (*intra*-psychological). This applies equally to voluntary attention, to logical memory, and to the formation of concepts. All the higher psychological functions originate as actual relations between human individuals. (Vygotsky, 1978, p. 46)

Of course, Vygotsky is better known to many of us in education for his *zone of proximal development* (ZPD). This zone is defined by the difference between what a student can do unaided and what he or she can do with prompting or with scaffolding provided by an adult or by more competent peers. Thus the ZPD focuses on the potential of our students rather than on the reality of what they can do now. This means we should aim to move our students *beyond* where they are now in terms of intellectual and personal development. That is one of the many reasons that dialogue can be such an effective part of our pedagogy.

To return to Dewey and Lipman: Both of these philosophers of education emphasized the need to develop in students the following personal habits, abilities and attitudes:

1. An inquiring outlook coupled with an ability to articulate problems
2. A tendency to be intellectually proactive and persistent
3. A capacity for imaginative and adventurous thinking
4. A habit of exploring alternative possibilities
5. An ability to critically examine issues
6. A capacity for sound independent judgment

They also wrote about social habits and dispositions such as these:

7. Actively listening to others and trying to understand their viewpoints
8. Giving reasons for what you say and expecting the same of others
9. Exploring disagreements reasonably
10. Being generally cooperative and constructive

11. Being socially communicative and inclusive

12. Taking other people's feelings and concerns into account

These interlocking, individual and social outcomes build on the tradition of reflective education while mirroring John Dewey's vision of a more deeply democratic way of life. Together these form the intended outcomes of high-quality dialogue.

These brief remarks are meant to convey something of the theoretical background to what is otherwise a book oriented toward practical strategies. We hope that we've said enough here—and in the first two chapters—to alert you to the intellectual underpinnings. All the authors of this book have been teaching assistants, teachers or leaders—and sometimes all three. So we know how easy it is to lose sight of the larger perspective when we're so busy with the day-to-day life in schools. However, if you can take time to reflect on our theoretical remarks and bear them in mind as you try some of the strategies in this book, then the outcomes of your efforts will be greatly enhanced.

THE LANGUAGE OF LEARNING

Here are some of the terms we use in this book.

Activity structures: strategies for engaging pupils in collaborative dialogue.

Argumentation: seen as the pursuit of truth rather than simply "arguing." Includes opinion *and* reason, and is intended to be persuasive.

Cognitive conflict: broadly defined as the mental discomfort produced when confronted with new information that contradicts prior beliefs and ideas.

Concept: a general idea that groups things together according to accepted characteristics.

Cumulative talk: talk that is characterized by repetitions, confirmations and elaborations.

Dialogue: conversation and inquiry. Combines the sociability of conversation with the skills of framing questions and constructing answers.

Dialogue "moves": When people respond to others in a dialogue by asking for an example or questioning an assumption, we say they are making a "move."

Discussion: the action or process of talking about something and exchanging ideas.

Disputational talk: talk that is critical of individuals (and their ideas), focuses on differences, is competitive and is all about being seen to "win."

Exploratory talk: talk that is characterized by longer exchanges, use of questions, reflection, explanation and speculation.

Inquiry: a process of questioning ideas, information and assumptions and of augmenting knowledge, resolving doubt or solving a problem.

IRE: the IRE structure of classroom interaction is teacher *initiation*, student *response*, teacher *evaluation*. Teachers use this most common pattern of classroom talk to ensure that pupils remember what they already know. This is not what we mean by dialogue.

Language of reasoning: The words, phrases and concepts that structure thinking, discussion or writing of any complexity. They help people think about everything else.

Metacognition: Literally meaning "thinking about thinking," metacognition is an important part of dialogue. It encourages students to think about the way in which they are thinking, how they are using the strategies and how they might improve for next time.

Reflection: giving serious thought or consideration to a thought, idea or response.

Reformulation: paraphrasing what another person has said to invite her or him to verify or disclaim that interpretation.

Repertoire and judgment: teachers have a repertoire of learning strategies, with good judgment required to know when and how to use those strategies.

Restatement: a summary by one person of the words used by another person during a dialogue.

Social constructivism: learning as an active process with the emphasis on collaboration.

SOLO taxonomy: the Structure of Observed Learning Outcomes model describes levels of increasing complexity in understanding of subjects, originally proposed by John B. Biggs and K. Collis.

Universalizing: giving a universal character or application to something, especially something abstract.

Wii-FM: useful shorthand for reminding teachers to think on behalf of their students: **W**hat's **I**n **I**t—**F**or **M**e.

> "We define our identity always in dialogue with, sometimes in struggle against, the things our significant others want to see in us. Even after we outgrow some of these others—our parents, for instance—and they disappear from our lives, the conversation with them continues within us as long as we live."
>
> (Taylor, 1994)

WHY DIALOGUE?

1.0 • WHY DIALOGUE?

Dialogue is one of the best vehicles for learning how to think, how to be reasonable, how to make moral decisions and how to understand another person's point of view. It is supremely flexible, instructional, collaborative and rigorous. At its very best, dialogue is one of the best ways for participants to learn good habits of thinking.

Robin Alexander, a professor in the United Kingdom, is one of the main advocates for teaching through dialogue, with many influential publications to his name. In one of his books, *Towards Dialogic Teaching: Rethinking Classroom Talk* (2006), he makes the following argument:

> **Dialogue allows us as teachers, leaders or support staff to intervene in the learning process by giving instant feedback, guidance and challenge to our students.**

1. Dialogue is undervalued in many schools when compared with writing, reading and math.

2. Dialogue does not get in the way of "real" teaching. In fact, by comparing PISA and other international tests, Alexander shows it is possible to teach more through dialogue and yet still be "at or near the top" of the tables.

3. Dialogue is the foundation of learning because it allows interaction and engagement with knowledge and with the ideas of others. Through

At its best, dialogue is one of the best vehicles for teaching good habits of thinking.

Robin Alexander's research shows dialogue leads to gains in international tests such as PISA.

> Dialogue gives teachers a valuable insight into their students' beliefs, questions and misconceptions.

dialogue, teachers can most effectively intervene in the learning process by giving instant feedback, guidance and stimulation to learners.

4. Dialogue in education is a special kind of talk, in that it uses structured questioning to guide and prompt students' conceptual understanding.

Some of the other benefits of dialogue include the opportunity to ask appropriate questions, articulate problems and issues, imagine life's possibilities, see where things lead, evaluate alternatives, engage with each other and think collaboratively. A wide-scale improvement in such abilities would be no panacea, but can you think of many more significant educational achievements than these?

1.1 • REASONS FOR DIALOGUE 1: LEARNING *HOW* TO THINK

(James) In 2003, Jill and I attended an international conference in Bulgaria. The focus was Philosophy for Children. In addition to the two hundred delegates from around the world, the organizers also invited some local teenagers to take part in proceedings. Midway through the four-day event, I was asked to facilitate a community of inquiry with these teenagers for the other delegates to observe.

I began the session with a fictional story about two hunters, Hank and Frank, who are chased by a talking bear. The teenagers then created a number of philosophical questions from which they chose their favorite: Why sacrifice yourself for others? After a short pause for quiet reflection, I invited an eager young man to start us off by giving his first thoughts. This is what he said:

> It seems to me that "sacrifice" is the most important concept in this question. I think someone might sacrifice themselves based on instinct, impulse or intuition. Of course, two of these are in the cognitive domain and one is in the affective domain, so I suppose we need to determine which of these is more likely in any given situation before we can answer the question effectively.

All the other delegates were nodding approvingly at the boy's apparent confidence in thinking about and analyzing the concept of sacrifice. As for me, I was like a rabbit caught in the headlights; I certainly had not been expecting that response!

To grab some thinking time for myself, I asked the teenagers to decide what these terms—instinct, impulse and intuition—had in common. While they did that, I asked a friendly philosopher to suggest what I might do next.

Reconvening, I asked one girl to give her group's answer. She will forevermore be a favorite of mine after replying: "Instinct, impulse and intuition have one thing in common . . . they are all names of perfumes." (At last: someone on my wavelength!)

Once the hour-long discussion had finished, I made a beeline for the organizers and moaned that they had staged all this: "You could've told me you'd invited only the most talented philosophers from across Bulgaria to join us!" They laughingly explained they had simply invited volunteers from the local area to take part—there had been no selection process.

"So how come they're so adept at thinking?" I inquired.

"Because they've been taught how to think from an early age," they said.

"But so have children in the United Kingdom, and yet I haven't come across young teenagers as skilled in thinking as your students," I countered.

Their response was something that initially vexed, then intrigued and ultimately emboldened me: "From what we've seen in Western countries, you don't seem to teach children *how* to think; instead you only teach them *what* to think."

The more I work in schools around the world, the more I think these Bulgarian teachers may have been right.

For example, if I ask children at the end of primary school (nine- to eleven- year-olds) if they think stealing is wrong, they all answer yes. But if I then ask why Robin Hood is thought of as a good man if stealing is wrong, they always retort: "Because he robbed from the rich and gave to the poor." Perhaps there's nothing too controversial there yet, but if I press them to decide if it would be okay for me to steal, let's say from a bank, and give the proceeds to poor people, they almost always say yes. Rarely do the children seem troubled by the fact that stealing from anybody, no matter what the funds are used for, is against the law.

I wonder if this suggests the Bulgarian teachers might be right—that too many children are being taught *what*, rather than *how*, to think.

Yet teaching students how to think feels like something of an abstract concept. Perhaps the simplest way to picture it is to consider one strategy for thinking that we all use when faced with a difficult choice: to list advantages and disadvantages. Creating this structure in our head is common to all of us. But it is not a structure we were born with— we were taught it, and it has become one of our "thinking tools." Dialogue allows us to model structures for thinking, for example, by asking questions, giving counter-examples, asking for reasons, justifying answers, adding to the last idea you heard. All of these are new thinking structures, and you are explicitly modeling and teaching them with students.

Another example: I often notice teachers and parents praising children for saying the "right" thing: "it is wrong to kill," "we must always be nice," "you should never lie" and so on. And on the face of it, this might seem reasonable. After all, we want children to be moral and to do the right thing. However, what happens if they are faced with a dilemma but, up to that point, have only ever followed instructions? Such dilemmas might include eating meat while maintaining that killing is wrong, always telling the truth even if it is likely to hurt someone, always being nice even to someone who is either being racist or bullying a friend. What then?

Many parents will reply that they trust their children to do the right thing. But how do children know what the "right" thing is unless they have learned how to make moral decisions for themselves? In other words, how can they be moral if they haven't learned *how* to think or developed at least some wisdom?

This is where dialogue comes in because it is one of the best ways to learn how to think, how to be reasonable, how to make moral decisions and how to understand another person's point of view. It is supremely flexible, instructional, collaborative and rigorous. At its very best, dialogue is arguably the best way for students to learn good habits of thinking.

For examples of teaching students how to think, look at the strategies in Chapter 4.

> Students benefit from being taught *how* to think, and dialogue is one of the best ways to achieve this.

> Dialogue can help to develop students' wisdom and ethics.

1.2 • REASONS FOR DIALOGUE 2: FROM SURFACE TO DEEP

(Jill) A lot of our teaching leads to students gaining some surface-level knowledge. Without this, many students would not "know" their numbers and letters or the myriad of subject-specific facts such as "rain is a form of precipitation."

However, our teaching does not often lead to students' deep understanding—at least not teaching in the traditional sense of "I speak and show; my students listen and learn."

This is not to criticize what teachers do: knowledge is a necessary first step to understanding. So helping students to gain some initial surface-level knowledge is an important function of our pedagogy.

Students *also* need to develop a deep understanding of concepts, connections, context and generalizations. There are many ways to achieve this, of which high-quality dialogue is one of the best.

> **Of course, the emphasis is on *high-quality* dialogue. Not just any old dialogue will do. High-quality dialogue includes getting students to generate ideas, create meaning, classify, compare, make links, question assumptions, test cause and effect, speculate, hypothesize and so on.**

Dialogue helps students to understand concepts, connections, context and general principles.

A very useful way to distinguish between surface-level knowledge and deep understanding is through the SOLO taxonomy. The Structure of Observed Learning Outcomes (SOLO) taxonomy (Martin, 2011) is a model that describes levels of increasing complexity in students' understanding of subjects. It was proposed by John B. Biggs and K. Collis and has since gained popularity.

We have written about the SOLO taxonomy in depth in *Challenging Learning Through Feedback* (Nottingham & Nottingham, 2016). We give an overview of it in Section 8.5 and suggest it as a way to review the outcomes of a mystery (one of the dialogue activities suggested in Chapter 8; see Figure 11 in Chapter 8).

The levels of the SOLO taxonomy are shown below. The bolded terms are the ones originally proposed by Biggs and Collis. The terms in brackets are the ones we find more useful when talking with students about the SOLO taxonomy.

The SOLO taxonomy provides a clear structure for thinking about how to deepen and extend dialogue.

1. **Prestructural** (NO IDEA): students have acquired bits of unconnected information, which have no organization and make no sense.

2. **Unistructural** (ONE IDEA): students have one or two correct pieces of information and have made simple connections between them. They do not grasp the significance of this information, though.

3. **Multistructural** (MANY IDEAS): students know a number of related facts and are able to connect them correctly. They do not yet understand the overall significance.

4. **Relational** (RELATE): students are now able to appreciate the significance of the parts in relation to the whole.

5. **Extended Abstract** (EXTEND): students are making connections within the given subject area and beyond it. They are also able to generalize and transfer the principles and ideas underlying the specific instance.

As you can see, the SOLO taxonomy provides a clear structure for thinking about understanding. Level 1 represents no knowledge at all; Levels 2 and 3 represent knowledge; Levels 4 and 5 represent understanding.

So in SOLO taxonomy terms, high-quality dialogue can help students move from Levels 2 and 3 to Levels 4 and 5.

That is what we aim to show you in this book: how to create the high-quality dialogue that can lead to this movement from surface-level knowledge to deep understanding.

1.3 • REASONS FOR DIALOGUE 3: CREATING A CLIMATE OF TRUST

(Richard Kielty) Trust is the firm belief in a person's reliability, benevolence and honesty. Research by Bryk and Schneider (2002) among others has shown that nurturing trusting relationships between teacher and students is a key element in improving student learning.

Building relational trust is about creating a learning environment in which students feel they can take risks, make mistakes, express opinions and collaborate. These are also necessary conditions for high-quality dialogue. So as teachers, we need to create a climate of respect and trust that allows for this expression—and to model how this can be done.

An effective dialogue should be like a handball match in which the teacher is just *one* of the players rather than the whole of the opposition team! The "ball" should be passed from teacher to student to another student to another and another and another before going back to the teacher and back again to another student and so on. Yet many dialogues in classrooms seem more like a tennis match with the "ball" going from teacher to student to teacher to another student and so on.

> Dialogue works best when the participants trust and respect each other.

As teachers we model how to respond to dialogue through how we respond to student answers. We show how to reflect, how to treat answers with respect and when to offer support. We also show how to deal with unconventional ideas. I am sure we can all remember a time when a student has expressed an idea that seemed so bizarre and out of the ordinary that other students laughed. Were they laughing at the idea or at the student for expressing the idea? How we respond to this type of situation establishes the tone for future discussions. I have seen students humiliated when teachers join in with the other students in laughing at them. It is unlikely that the humiliated student will contribute any further ideas willingly and confidently. Instead, the idea given could and should have been used to stimulate discussion and to challenge misconceptions.

> The way in which a teacher listens, invites and responds sets the expectations for how students should also behave during a dialogue.

As a teacher, I might feed additional information to students and encourage them to rethink their ideas. I would acknowledge and value the fact that students are willing to take risks when answering questions and encourage them to build on risky answers. When modeling effective dialogue, we should prompt responses but not shape them (e.g., Does anyone have anything to add? Does anyone disagree with that?).

Opening a dialogue with students about the meaning and importance of trust is a valuable exercise in helping build a classroom culture that is inclusive, empathetic and safe. Everyone has experience with trust and can speak about the impact of its presence or absence in a variety of contexts and relationships. Making an explicit link between the development of specific character traits and the individual's contribution to the group within a classroom is essential for students to develop a sense of belonging. When students feel this sense of belonging, then dialogue becomes authentic and meaningful. This then leads to deeper understanding of ideas and concepts.

1.4 • REASONS FOR DIALOGUE 4: DEVELOPING LANGUAGE TO EXPRESS UNDERSTANDING

(Martin) A few years ago, I was faced with one of the most awkward moments of my teaching career, when I was asked if someone could record one of my lessons for a piece of research they were doing at a local university.

As you can imagine, I felt rather anxious about someone putting a camera in my classroom. How would the students react? What would I see on film that I wasn't aware of in the room? What would I do and say that might be embarrassing? And worst of all, would the camera notice I have a double chin and show that I'm thinning a bit on top?

The purpose of the video was to record examples of teacher questioning and classroom dialogue, to investigate the amount—and type—of student talk taking place in the classroom. The university researcher (let's call her "Alan"), was focusing on the amount of time students spent engaged in talk, how much time they had to think about responses and the balance of the type and purpose of the questions asked in the room. Her research was in fact based on that conducted by Mary Budd Rowe back in 1972, focusing on teacher questions. Alan was trying to find out if the modern classroom was any different (Rowe, 1986).

> Mary Budd Rowe's research showed that the typical wait time between a teacher asking a question and either a student answering or the teacher continuing to talk is just 0.8 seconds!

Budd Rowe's original research drew conclusions about talk in classrooms that reveal some startling statistics about dialogue and thinking. She observed that after asking a question, the typical amount of wait time before the teacher either took an answer from the students or continued talking was around 0.8 seconds. Yes, you read that correctly: 0.8 seconds! That's less than 1 second for a student to think of a response before someone else shouts out an answer or the teacher moves on to talk about something else.

Is it really any wonder that students become disengaged? It doesn't sound like a game worth joining, does it?

From the students' perspective, here's how that game looks:

Teacher: In which year did the Vikings first invade Britain?

Student: (thinking to herself, "*I know this one, it's . . .*")

      Meanwhile Mary shouts out the answer.

Teacher: That's right, Mary. Thank you. As we were talking about yesterday, the Vikings first landed here in 793.

Student: (thinking to herself, "*Oh, so it was 793 not 795.*")

      Meanwhile the teacher asks another question.

Teacher: Can anyone remember where in Britain the Vikings first landed?

Student: (still thinking about 793 or 795, but now starting to think about the next question)

Teacher (less than 1 second after asking the previous question): It was Lindisfarne in the Kingdom of Northumbria.

Student: (thinking to herself, "What did he just say about Northumbria?")

You will notice a strong correlation here between this example of classroom talk and the IRE pattern that we cover in the next chapter. In this kind of conversation, the typical length of a student answer is only 1.3 seconds. This is because of the expectation placed on the student that this pattern of talk creates: "I ask, you respond, I move on." This pattern soon becomes a habit in classrooms for both the teacher and the student.

When I first heard about Budd Rowe's research, I was rather skeptical; surely we can't just leave a wait time of only 0.8 seconds before taking an answer or moving on? And surely the student talks for more than 1.3 seconds.

Yet, when I watched the video of my own practice—even though I am experienced in teaching dialogue—there were many questions I asked that were either answered by me or answered in very quick time (sometimes before I'd even finished asking the question!). Or when students did answer, it was the usual suspects who answered.

> Budd Rowe's work suggests a very simple way to improve dialogue, which is to introduce wait time. She observed that when the teacher waits for a minimum of 3 seconds *before* taking an answer from the students, and then waits another 3 seconds *after* taking an answer from the students, the effects in the classroom are staggering:
>
> - **The length of explanations increases fivefold among advantaged groups and sevenfold among disadvantaged groups.**
>
> - **The number of volunteered, appropriate answers by larger numbers of students greatly increases.**
>
> - **Failures to respond and "I don't know" responses decrease from 30 percent to less than 5 percent.**
>
> - **The number of questions asked by children rises.**
>
> - **Students' scores on academic achievement tests show a tendency to increase.**

> There are many advantages for students when the wait time between question and response is increased to 3 or more seconds.

There are also benefits in wait time for teachers' practice too. When teachers wait 3 seconds at appropriate times in the dialogue, the following happen:

- Their questioning strategies tend to be more varied and flexible.

- They decrease the quantity and increase the quality (and variety) of their questions.

- They ask additional questions that require more complex information processing and higher-level thinking on the part of students.

You can find out more about specific questioning techniques and their role in dialogue in our book *Challenging Learning Through Questioning* (Nottingham & Renton, in press).

> Extending wait time also improves the quality and variety of teachers' questions.

Budd Rowe's research has been repeated many times over in many different countries since 1972, and the results are consistent: in the typical classroom students get very little time to process information, language and ideas in order to be able to contribute to a dialogue.

Stahl's (1990) update of the work coined the term *think time* to describe what was happening in the 3 seconds, to demonstrate that students are actively processing, rather than simply waiting. This small alteration is a powerful one in changing our practice in dialogue, suggesting that students are contributing even when not speaking, because they are involved in active, internal dialogue.

Following my video experience, I regularly use the strategy Think-Pair-Share as a very simple reminder that students need time to think, to process their ideas and, most important, to practice the language needed to contribute to the dialogue.

> Think-Pair-Share is an effective tool for increasing wait time. It also gives students more opportunity to develop their language of learning.

In the example conversation earlier, the only person really practicing any subject-specific vocabulary is the teacher—and teachers are not the ones who need the practice! Think-Pair-Share allows that practice, both internally and verbally. After asking a question, the teacher gives think time (a minimum of 3 seconds) so the students can begin constructing a response independently. The students then pair up and talk to one another about their possible answers. The pairs are then invited to share their answer with the class.

- Ask a question.
- **Think** on your own for a minimum of 3 seconds.
- In a **pair** discuss your possible answers.
- **Share** your ideas with the class.

The advantage to this approach is that the students get ample opportunity to prepare and practice the language they need before answering the question. By preparing independently first, then verbalizing their ideas, then comparing with another student's ideas, they have time to rehearse and formulate their ideas. This in turn often leads to students being more willing to contribute their ideas, more able to use the subject language and more willing to take a risk in being wrong.

The Think-Pair-Share pattern is a very good way to model structured thinking, help the students engage and contribute, create an ethos of risk-taking and support progress. At the heart of this is the development, processing and rehearsal of language.

1.5 • REVIEW

This chapter has covered the following main points:

1. Dialogue is one of the best vehicles for learning how to think, how to be reasonable, how to make moral decisions and how to understand another person's point of view.

2. Dialogue is supremely flexible, instructional, collaborative and rigorous. At its very best, dialogue is one of the best ways for participants to learn good habits of thinking.

3. Dialogue does not get in the way of "real" teaching. It *is* possible to teach more through dialogue and yet still be "at or near the top" of the tables.

4. Dialogue helps participants to learn *how* to think as well as *what* to think.

5. Dialogue helps students to move from surface-level knowledge through to deep understanding of concepts.

6. Dialogue can develop a climate of trust and support.

7. Dialogue develops language and helps participants know how to better express their ideas and understanding.

1.6 • NEXT STEPS

Here are some suggestions to help you with your reflections on dialogue:

1. Pay attention to the types of talk that take place in your classroom: Which interactions would you class as conversation and which as dialogue?

2. Do some of your students lean more toward dialogue than toward conversation? If so, what attitudes and skills do they bring to this?

3. Are there some common features between dialogue in different disciplines? For example, between scientific dialogues and dialogues examining literature?

4. How often do you use dialogue with your students?

5. What are the benefits?

6. What problems do you encounter?

> "A dialogue is very important. It is a form of communication in which question and answer continue until a question is left without an answer."
>
> (Krishnamurti, 1989)
> Described by the Dalai Lama as one of the greatest thinkers of the age

DIALOGUE ESSENTIALS

2.0 • DIALOGUE BASICS

In the most basic sense, dialogue is the to and fro of talk between people who want to be understood.

Dialogue is NOT:

Dialogue is not just "conversation." Whereas a conversation might go nowhere (or indeed *any*where), a dialogue properly defined and conducted always goes *some*where (for example, answering or examining a key question that was identified in the early stages of the dialogue).

Dialogue is not some mystical thing reserved for those with training. Having said that, there *are* processes and judgment calls that can be developed in order to enhance the quality and effect of dialogue. That is what this book seeks to help you with: to both develop your repertoire in using dialogue and encourage you to reflect on your practice so that your judgment of how, when and what to do when using dialogue leads to enhanced learning outcomes.

Dialogue doesn't take place just in education. The moment parents respond to their child's first sounds and engages them both in a communicative relationship, the foundations for dialogue are being built.

Dialogue isn't just *between* people; it also takes place *within* people in that thinking is rather like an inner dialogue. At least some forms of thinking are. Perhaps not the subconscious, automatic type of thinking but certainly the reflective, ponderous form of thinking can be said to be an internal dialogue. This makes dialogue all the more important. If the patterns of talk established

> Dialogue is not just "conversation." Often conversation does not go anywhere, whereas dialogue should always go somewhere.

in communication with others influence our patterns of internal dialogue, then dialogue leads to thinking itself.

Dialogue is not the Initiate-Response-Evaluate (IRE) model of questioning that is used in many classrooms. IRE is a teacher-led, three-part sequence that begins with the teacher asking a student a question or introducing a topic for the purpose of finding out whether the student knows an answer. Though this style of questioning does have some place in education, it is only really a way of checking students' factual recall. It tends not to be very productive in terms of higher-order thinking nor particularly useful for dialogue. Even if a higher-order question is posed, generally only one student gets to answer the question before the teacher evaluates the answer and ends any form of discussion.

> Dialogue is not debate. Dialogue focuses more on inquiry and constructing understanding. Debate focuses more on polarization and persuasion.

Dialogue is not debate. Though many people use the term *debate* when talking about dialogue, they are not one and the same thing. Debate is a type of classroom talk that, like IRE and conversation, has its purpose and benefits, but also its limitations. In debate, the situation is typically set up to create polarised views—usually a "for" and "against" group, with participants encouraged to express opinions that support only their side of the argument. Sometimes the students talk as themselves, and sometimes they are asked to take the role of someone else (a character from a book or from history, for example).

Debate encourages students to give reasons, to talk for an extended period, to participate and to use the language of persuasion.

However, debate has its drawbacks because it is a form of disputational talk (see Section 2.6.2). The main purpose of debate is to win the battle and persuade others to agree with a particular view. This means that students may not listen properly to opposing points of view and instead just present their own perspective. There might also be less value placed on co-constructing new understanding or preparing counter-argument and more emphasis on preparing winning statements or assertions.

That is not to say that debate does not have a purpose in education; of course it does. However, to ensure that debate is meaningful, opportunities for reflection need to be regular, constant and focused on the strength of reasons given and the challenges made. The students need to know explicitly that the arguments presented are part of the learning process.

Dialogue IS:

> **Dialogue is conversation *and* inquiry. Dialogue combines the sociability of conversation with the skills of framing questions and constructing answers.**

> Dialogue should motivate and engage students as well as deepen their understanding of concepts and connections.

Dialogue is about working collaboratively to understand what has not yet been understood and to form reasoned judgments and inferences. The IRE structure is compatible with dialogue, but it is not the *same* as dialogue. Dialogue can take participants further. It can help your students become capable thinkers, willing and able to learn, reason and express themselves clearly and confidently. At its best, dialogue will also foster encouragement, engagement, understanding and exploration.

Dialogue is a supremely flexible and stimulating instrument of thought. As children get older, the issues they need to understand, the judgments they need to make and the relationships they need to maintain become more complex. The turn-taking structure of dialogue that leads a child to learn the rudiments of language also serves as a means of thinking about complex issues. Thus dialogue is holistic in its intentions *and* its outcomes.

2.1 • PUTTING DIALOGUE IN THE CONTEXT OF EDUCATIONAL OBJECTIVES

If we asked you "What is education?" you would probably have a very clear view and could give an answer. You might say, for example, that education is the formal process of learning in school. But if we asked another person in your school the same question, he or she might give a different answer, for example, that education is developing the skills needed for lifelong learning. Another person in your school might say it is an opportunity that opens doors, and so on.

All of these ideas are valid; there are, of course, many answers to the same question. If you put all of those ideas together, you have then created a group sense of what education is, using your own language to express the thinking.

Now if we look at research from across the world about characteristics of great lessons, we'd find an extremely long list of elements, including the following:

- active listening

- learning intentions connected to attitudes, skills and knowledge

- students struggling and persevering

- appropriate resources that stimulate learning

- students working on individualized tasks

- students actively engaged in the direction of learning with a degree of ownership

- students questioning each other and the teacher

- phrases and comments that search for better understanding

- creative ideas being expressed and/or formed

- students talking about the learning process (e.g., What am I learning? How much progress have I made? What are my next learning steps?)

To make these (and all the other factors you might add to the list) more manageable, consider the headings or umbrella terms under which all of these elements can sit. We find the following list useful in this regard:

Learning should be:

Active (so your students are exploring their own ideas)

Meaningful (so your students make connections and access knowledge)

Challenging (so your students have to think)

Collaborative (so your students work together and share ideas)

Mediated (so you are guiding rather than telling)

Reflective (so your students have time to think about what they have learned)

> High-quality dialogue is active, meaningful, challenging, collaborative, mediated and reflective.

Planning lessons around all, or a combination of any, of these key elements is likely to produce an engaging and successful session. Such a lesson would feature lots of shared talk, questioning, exploration of ideas, reflection on learning and student thinking.

A high-quality dialogue with your students will give you exactly that!

As you try the activities in this book with your students, see if you can make connections back to the six elements above. Were your learners exploring their own ideas; making connections to their own knowledge; thinking and struggling; sharing ideas and opinions; being prompted by the teacher; thinking about how others' views might influence, or add to, their own understanding?

2.2 • THE HIDDEN CLASSROOM

Professor Graham Nuthall spent years recording and evaluating classroom dialogue by putting microphones on every student in the schools he researched. He used this approach because his early research had led him to conclude that up to 40 percent of what happened among students was missed by observations and whole-class recordings.

Nuthall (2007) shared his findings in *The Hidden Lives of Learners*. In it he stated:

> Graham Nuthall's research shows that one-third of the learning each individual student acquires is not learned by anyone else. Dialogue provides an opportunity for students to share their unique insights with each other.

1. Students live in a personal and social world of their own.

2. Students already know at least 40 percent of what teachers have planned for them to learn.

3. A third of what each student learns is not learned by any other student in the class.

4. Students learn how and when the teacher will notice them and how to give the appearance of active involvement.

5. A quarter of the specific concepts and principles that students learn are critically dependent on private peer talk.

These five points in themselves are a strong justification for increasing the quantity and quality of dialogue in education.

Dialogue should help us as teachers understand the personal and social world of students. It should give us better insight into what our students already know so that we can plan lessons more accurately. It can provide a better opportunity for students to share with each other their own, and often unique, insights. It should cause students to be less concerned about *pretending* to be actively involved and actually help them to *be* engaged. And it should continue to help students process and understand concepts and principles—only this time it will be to the benefit of many others in the group and not just to the student's immediate peer(s).

When teachers focus on using strategies for dialogue for the first time, they often observe that they learned more about the students during that short episode than they had in the whole academic year to that point. That is because dialogue is less about the answer itself and more about the reasons behind the answer.

However, we often find it hard to create opportunities for open-ended dialogue during a lesson and easily become trapped in the IRE pattern of talk. There is a simple reason for this: dialogue is not a natural form of talk and doesn't always come easily to us or to our students. When we leave dialogue to chance and make it up on the spur of the moment, it often becomes IRE. In reality, good dialogue requires planning and focused opportunities to make sure that it really happens in the classroom.

2.3 • ACTIVE ENGAGEMENT

In his visible learning research, John Hattie (2011) observed that in a typical classroom, the person working the hardest is the teacher, and most of the classroom talk is done by (you guessed it) the teacher. Indeed, Hattie noted that one of the outcomes of reducing class size is that teachers of smaller classes talk even more!

This, of course, is a crazy state of affairs and needs to change. Students need to be more active!

Students should be *actively* thinking about what they are being taught, comparing this with prior learning, making connections to other experiences and sharing their ideas with others who may have understood it differently.

Student dialogue allows them not only to explore concepts more deeply but also to develop the language they need to express their understanding in their own terms. The more they develop a language to express their understanding, the better they become at processing information and therefore the more they express their understanding. There is a clear cycle of progress that comes from cognition and expressing ideas in language.

> John Hattie's analysis of 65,000 studies shows that in the typical classroom, it is the teacher who works hardest. Dialogue can restore the balance and get students working harder.

2.4 • CONDITIONS FOR SUCCESSFUL DIALOGUE

In the Introduction we shared the attitudes, dispositions and abilities that Dewey and Lipman declared were crucial for high-quality dialogue. These would be worth sharing with older students. However, if you work with younger students then perhaps you could start with the following conditions for successful dialogue:

1. **Dialogue should challenge our ideas, reasons and assumptions.**

2. **Dialogue should make us wobble.**

3. **We don't always have to arrive at an answer; the dialogue is just as important as the end result.**

4. **We co-construct meaning by accepting that all responses have meaning, are valid and are valuable.**

2.5 • LANGUAGE FOR DIALOGUE

Throughout this book, you will find recommendations for ways to improve the quality of dialogue. One of the best ways to start is by considering the concepts and actions you want to encourage your students to use. These might include those shown in Figure 1.

▶ Figure 1: **Concepts and Actions in High-Quality Dialogue**

Type of Thinking	Dialogue "Moves"	Concepts
Productive	Generating ideas, generating alternative ideas, listing	Alternative, list, collection, class, category
Collaborative	Listening, taking turns, suspending judgment, establishing and applying ground rules	Community
Creating meaning	Questioning, classifying, comparing, ranking, connecting, clarifying, exemplifying, offering analogies, interpreting, summarizing, defining, elaborating	Same, different, principle, example, important, significant, special, ordinary, function, purpose, part, whole, multiple, single, complete, incomplete, class, category, all, some, none, many
Argumentative (Argument is seen as the pursuit of truth rather than simply "arguing" as children might argue over a toy.)	Agreeing, disagreeing, making an argument, questioning assumptions, assessing evidence	Opinion, belief, proposition, conclusion, claim, reason, premise, argument, cause, effect, symptom, consequence, true or false, agree, disagree, doubt, class, category, all, some, none, many, assumption, evidence, criteria, proof, judgment, justify
Speculative	Hypothesizing, predicting, imagining, offering thought experiments	Cause, effect, symptom, consequence, theory, hypothesis

2.6 • EXPLORATORY TALK

> Neil Mercer's research shows that exploratory talk is the most effective for learning because it engages critical and constructive thinking.

Neil Mercer described three types of talk that typically happen in the classroom: cumulative talk, disputational talk and exploratory talk. Of these three, Mercer identified exploratory talk as the most powerful for student learning. He explains exploratory talk as

> that in which partners engage critically but constructively with each other's ideas. Relevant information is offered for joint consideration. Proposals may be challenged and counter-challenged, but if so reasons are given and alternatives are offered. Agreement is sought as a basis for joint progress. Knowledge is made publicly accountable and reasoning is visible in the talk. (Mercer, 2000b, p. 98)

Consider the key phrases in the Mercer quote that refer to powerful learning: *joint consideration, counter-challenge, reasoning, alternatives offered, agreement, joint progress.* All of these are fundamentally related to a classroom ethos whereby learning takes place through dialogue and students not only are challenged but expect to be challenged as well.

However, when Rupert Wegerif (2002) looked into the types of talk found in classrooms, he discovered very little exploratory talk occurs when students work together in groups. Instead the less learning-focused types of talk predominate, and students more naturally lean toward disputational or cumulative talk.

Before we look at how to best develop and use exploratory talk in your classroom, let's examine what these other two types are.

2.6.1 • Cumulative Talk

This type of talk is typically heard when friendship groups work together or when an unfamiliar group is getting to know each other. The talk is positive and affirming, making everyone feel included and welcome. The participants rarely criticize each other or the ideas being put forward. Not everyone in the group takes part, nor are they expected to. The group accepts first ideas and does not try to go beyond these. This leads to an accumulation of "common knowledge" and a sense of "harmony in the group."

Cumulative talk is characterized by repetitions, confirmations and elaborations.

(Martin) Here's an example from a group of twelve-year-olds I worked with recently. Four students were looking at a map together and trying to decide where the best place is to build a settlement:

> **Student 1:** I think [this] is the best place. (*points to the map*)
>
> **Student 2:** Yeah, me too. I would go with that because it's near the river and the trees.
>
> **Student 3:** Good idea. That makes it safe, and they've got water to drink.
>
> **Student 2:** And wood for building.
>
> **Student 4:** (*nods*)
>
> **Student 1:** Excellent. So we all agree on this choice?
>
> **All:**   Yes! (*high fives all round*)

Cumulative talk such as this dialogue might seem good. The students developed a positive atmosphere, gave some reasons for their ideas *and* reached consensus. The problem is there was no challenge, no rethinking of the first assumption and no critical or creative thinking. There was no consideration of an alternative place to build and no disadvantages given for the chosen site, and none of the reasons for building were explored further. In reality, the reasons given were rather vague and in one case incorrect: the "river" they had chosen was actually salt water, but no one challenged the notion. The students went with their first idea and played it safe. Although there was a sense of harmony in the group, there was very little learning going on.

What do you notice about this type of talk? Is it something you hear often in the classroom? What are the positive elements of this type of talk, and does it promote progress and good learning?

2.6.2 • Disputational Talk

This type of talk is less prevalent than you might think and is actually quite hard to spot because it can occur under the radar. It is much more negative than cumulative talk.

However, Rupert Wegerif found that very little exploratory talk takes place in classrooms.

Cumulative talk is more common in classrooms. It is characterized by agreeable and affirming "moves" with very little critical thought.

Disputational talk is less common but is critical of individuals, focuses on differences and is all about being seen to win.

Disputational talk is critical of individuals (and their ideas), focuses on differences, is competitive and is all about being seen to win. The group do not work together nor pool their resources/intellect. Individuals within the group dominate. Mistakes are criticized and perhaps even ridiculed.

Disputational talk is characterized by short interactions, there is little attempt to listen to each other and the talk is dominated by assertions and counter-assertions.

(Martin) This is an example recorded on a video I made with a group of eleven-year-olds during a technology lesson in which they were discussing their design for a toy car. There were three students in the group.

> **Student 1:** We'll put big wheels at the back, and we'll paint skulls on the front.
>
> **Student 2:** I hate drag racers. Can we not make it like a Ferrari?
>
> **Student 1:** Don't be stupid—we're making it out of wood. How's it going to look like a Ferrari, you idiot?
>
> **Student 2:** But drag racers are ugly . . .
>
> **Student 1:** No, they're not . . .
>
> **Student 2:** They are!
>
> **Student 1:** Well, I don't think so.
> (*silence for a few seconds*)
>
> **Student 2:** Anyway, we haven't got any bigger wheels.
>
> **Student 1:** We can get some—that's easy.
>
> **Student 2:** Look, just change this bit here. (*starts to erase some of the design on paper*)
>
> **Student 3:** Get off, man! Don't ruin it. I'm not starting again! You're being stupid. (*shouting across to the teacher*) Miss, he's spoiling our work.

The students in this group sound like they are misbehaving. In fact, they were engaged in the task of building the car and talking about the design, and they were sharing ideas about how they wanted it to look. They were not, however, being productive or getting the best from the task because they were not making any effort to work together. Their focus was on ensuring that their individual design was the one chosen for the car. They were not interested in compromise, so progress was hampered by criticisms and bad feelings.

What do you notice about this type of talk? Is it something you hear often in the classroom, or is it a type of talk we often miss? Are there any positive elements in this type of talk, or is it always negative?

2.6.3 • Exploratory Talk

Exploratory talk is characterized by longer exchanges and use of questions, reflection, explanation and speculation. It should make full use of critical thinking as well as be very creative.

To make best use of the approach, your students should explore ideas and offer reasons for their thinking; they should expect to be challenged by other students. Any challenges they make should be accompanied by reasons so that the whole group can learn from the interaction. There should be no risk of losing face if they get it "wrong" because all statements should be offered in the expectation of helping everyone make progress. The connection between this type of talk and improved language skills, both in general

Exploratory talk is the most productive for learning. It involves longer exchanges, more questions and reflection, and is speculative and inquiry-led.

and in subject-specific terms, should become apparent as your students process the information at their own level and then seek to go beyond it.

Achieve this, and the results can be very impressive.

> Wegerif and Scrimshaw (1997) studied the impact of the explicit teaching of exploratory talk on nine- and ten-year-old students. They found that after five weeks of using exploratory talk, the number of questions students asked each other increased from seventeen to eighty-six, the number of reasons given more than doubled and the number of speculations (what if . . .) rose from two to thirty-five. In total, the number of words used by the groups almost doubled.
>
> Wegerif and Scrimshaw concluded that the explicit teaching of exploratory talk led to an improvement in the quality and variety of language used by groups as well as to an improvement in individual performance of the students in the groups. This suggests a strong connection between social interaction (thinking together) and improved cognitive development.

The example below is from a group of twelve-year-old students in a science lesson. They were trying to build a bridge to carry a toy car across a river, using a set of materials provided by the teacher. They had two blocks and a piece of paper to build with:

Student 1: Well, first, I think we need to know how big the bridge has to be.

Student 2: We could measure the width of the river. I'll do that.

Student 1: Okay. Do we need to draw a plan?

Student 3: We can just try it out and see what happens. Look, what about putting the blocks here with the paper over the top, like that? (*balances paper across the blocks*)

Student 1: That's not going to work, is it? (*places car on paper bridge*) See? It just collapses. Paper's not strong enough to hold up the car. Is there a different way we could do it?

(*silence as students think*)

Student 2: The bridge only needs to be 15 cm. So it's not that long . . . and we don't need all that paper . . . so . . . can we tear it?

Student 3: How would that help?

Student 2: It wouldn't be as big as this (*demonstrates large surface area with hand movements*), so it wouldn't be as floppy, 'cause it's not as wide. If it's thinner it's not going to wobble around as much, maybe?

Student 1: Do you think? What if . . . you tear it . . . then put the two pieces on top of each other. Would that work? Try it, look!

Students 3 & 4: No!

Student 3: Wait! (*grabs paper*) We've only got one piece of paper. We should work it out first, rather than just being random. We're meant to know our reasons why . . . for why we did it this way. If we fold it like that . . . it's double-thickness, so it should be stronger. Is that going to work? (*reaches for toy car*)

Student 1:   We can fold it, and fold it again, so it's really narrow. But really thick. See? It's quite dense in the middle. That shouldn't bend as much now when the car's on it. But what do you think? (*tries the bridge, but it bends so much the car is in the river*) Oh well, that didn't work.

Student 4:   But folding it seems to be better. It's stronger. Didn't we say [in the last lesson] that triangles are a strong shape? How can we fold it into triangles? 'Cause that'll make it hold the car. I don't know how [to fold it], though. Where would the triangles come from? Can we get more paper and try folding it more?

When compared with the example of disputational talk (see Section 2.6.2), you can see that reasons are now offered, explanations are longer, questions are asked and the students are speculating on the possibilities. The students in the group have listened to one another and are expressing their ideas. The students benefit from this shared language and are not seeking to prove that they are the winner. There is clear progress being made in their learning from the start to the end of the dialogue, and they are reaching a consensus about the best way forward.

What do you notice about this type of talk? Is it something you hear often in the classroom, and does it require the students to have any specific skills? Why might it not happen very often in the classroom, and what could we do to ensure it happens more?

2.6.4 • Making Exploratory Talk Happen

> Exploratory talk occurs in an environment in which students feel comfortable to explore ideas with, and to trust in, each other.

Exploratory talk occurs in an environment in which students feel comfortable to explore ideas with, and to trust in, each other. This means your students will need to recognize the benefit of collaborative learning and to know that when viewpoints are expressed, challenged or explored, it is always for the purpose of new understanding and not for point-scoring or the belittling of others.

Making this a reality in the classroom requires some careful planning and preparation. Kathryn Bullen and Kirsty Moore (1999) suggest creating an explicit set of ground rules, negotiated by the learners, to provide the structure they need for exploratory talk to flourish. Such ground rules can enhance the quality of the learning that takes place in the classroom.

We recommend that you involve your students in the creation of these ground rules. This will generate a greater sense of ownership on their part. It will also mean your students are more likely to understand the spirit as well as the letter of the rules. In Section 5.2 we share some recommendations for ground rules based on research carried out by Rupert Wegerif. You can give these to your students to edit or keep them up your sleeve in case your students are struggling for inspiration when creating their own set.

> Rules for dialogue can help to set the right tone and expectations for exploratory talk to flourish.

Remember: these are rules for talk. They are not the same as class rules for behavior. If you also have class rules, then they should be kept separate from the dialogue rules so that your students know the dialogue rules are there to help them learn how to talk with each other rather than learn how to behave. There might be some crossover, but it is important to keep each set of rules separate and distinct.

Below is a set of dialogue rules created by a class of nine- and ten-year-olds recently. Once agreed upon, these rules were printed out and used by each group as a reminder of how to engage with each other.

- Everyone should have a turn to speak.

- Don't interrupt when someone else is speaking.

- Try to answer what other people say.

- Accept advice and suggestions.

- Don't make others feel bad about what they say.

No matter how your dialogue rules are created, make sure you keep referring to them. This might feel unnecessary at times. However, Wegerif and others have found that a simple set of agreed-upon ground rules that are consistently referred to have far greater influence on improving the quality and focus of dialogues than rules that are established but not frequently referred to. This is particularly true when students are working in smaller collaborative groups.

2.7 • REVIEW

This chapter has covered the following main points:

1. Dialogue is conversation *and* inquiry. Dialogue combines the sociability of conversation with the skills of framing questions and constructing answers.

2. Dialogue is about working collaboratively to understand what has not yet been understood and to form reasoned judgments and inferences.

3. High-quality dialogue will be active, meaningful, challenging, collaborative, expertly mediated and reflective.

4. Dialogue should give us better insight into what our students already know so that we can plan lessons more accurately.

5. High-quality dialogue can help students move from surface-level knowledge to deep understanding of concepts.

6. The types of thinking developed in high-quality dialogue should include productive, collaborative, meaning-creating, argumentative and speculative thinking.

7. Exploratory talk is one of the most productive forms of dialogue.

8. Exploratory talk is characterized by longer exchanges, use of questions, reflection, explanation and speculation. It should make full use of critical thinking as well as be very creative.

2.8 • NEXT STEPS AND FURTHER READING

Here are some questions to help you with your reflections on dialogue:

1. Pay attention to the types of talk that take place in your classroom: which interactions would you class as conversation and which as dialogue?

2. How often do you use the IRE pattern of classroom talk? What happens to the dialogue after the E (evaluate)? Why does that happen?

3. What would happen if you changed the last step (E) and did something else, said something else or asked something else? What might that be?

4. You might try recording a lesson with a camera and watching your dialogue. What do you notice? How long did you leave for think time, and how long were the student answers?

5. Do some of your students lean more toward dialogue than toward conversation? If so, what attitudes and skills do they bring to this?

6. Is internal dialogue as valuable as verbal dialogue? How do you know when internal dialogue is taking place? Is it important to know when this is happening?

7. What forms of talk occur most often between your students: cumulative, disputational or exploratory?

You could also read one or more of the following books. We have included web links where they exist.

1. **How (Well-Structured) Talk Builds the Mind** (Resnick, Michaels & O'Connor, 2010)

    This book chapter includes good sections on "moves" for learning in classroom dialogues and the interesting and useful concept of accountable talk. Lauren Resnick, Sarah Michaels and M. C. O'Connor pose three aspects of accountability:

    1. Accountability to the learning community

    2. Accountability to standards of reasoning

    3. Accountability to knowledge

2. *The Guided Construction of Knowledge* (Mercer, 2000a)

    Neil Mercer has researched classroom dialogue for many years. His approach is based on the work of Russian psychologist Lev Vygotsky (1896–1934). This short book is about how one person helps another develop knowledge and understanding through dialogue. In particular, Mercer explains the language techniques used by teachers for developing a shared version of knowledge with their students. The book is also relevant to issues raised in Chapters 2 and 4.

    A related article by Mercer is available online at http://bit.ly/1xe2XRv.

3. *Challenging Learning* (Nottingham, 2016)

    Challenging Learning is an accessible, interesting and practical resource that will inspire great teaching and learning. There are lots of recommendations for developing high-quality dialogue and plenty of resources at the back of the book for helping you get started with dialogue.

> "In human societies there will always be differences of views and interests. But the reality today is that we are all interdependent and have to co-exist on this small planet. Therefore, the only sensible and intelligent way of resolving differences and clashes of interests, whether between individuals or nations, is through dialogue."
>
> (The Dalai Lama, 1997)

DIALOGUE TO ENGAGE STUDENTS

3.0 • PREVIEW

In this chapter, we show how the first step in a successful dialogue is to engage your students. Part of this involves showing your students you have confidence in them as capable dialogue partners.

We provide the following simple but powerful strategies for you to try in order to foster the engagement of students in their own learning:

- Adopt a stance of intellectual encouragement toward your students as outlined in Section 3.1.

- Invite students to voice their questions and ideas.

- Take written notes of what students say.

- In dialogue with students, use the strategies of restating or reformulating their words and asking them to respond.

3.1 • GETTING THE ETHOS RIGHT

The most important strategy for initiating fruitful dialogue is intellectual encouragement. Show your students that you regard them as thinkers who are capable (even if they need help) of contributing to their own learning by sharing their questions and ideas.

> Intellectual encouragement underpins high-quality dialogue.

Your encouraging stance should convey the following attitudes:

- **I am interested in and respect your ideas.**

- **I will show my interest by listening to you, questioning you and giving you feedback.**

- **I am confident you are the sort of person who can come up with relevant questions, opinions, reasons, examples and comparisons.**

- **I will work as much as I can with your questions, understandings, interests and values.**

- **I am creating a classroom community in which we are a group of thinkers who can tackle questions together and work toward the best answers and understandings.**

- **We should all feel secure enough to take intellectual risks.**

3.2 • ISSUING INVITATIONS

> It is best to start a dialogue by inviting participants to share their understandings, explanations, judgments, opinions, comparisons and connections.

After you have clarified the values of intellectual encouragement, interest and respect, then you are ready to initiate a dialogue. A great way to do this is to "issue invitations." This is when you ask your students, in pairs, to come up with questions or statements about what they believe to be the most important aspects of a topic and those they find most difficult to understand. Make notes on what they say in order to show your interest. Show students how to group questions and statements according to type, for example:

- understandings and explanations

- judgments and expressions of opinion

- comparisons and connections (with other topics and experiences).

Example Responses

(Jill) When working with some nine-year-olds recently, I was reviewing the previous lesson about telling time. Here are some of the comments and questions my students came up with:

1. I was getting annoyed because I didn't get it at all, 'cause it was all new and confusing.

2. I now understand how to tell the time with analog, digital and twenty-four-hour clock.

3. Telling the time is important because then you know when to meet someone (assuming you've arranged to meet someone at a particular time).

4. Telling the time is an important part of math.

5. When you start working, you will need to be able to tell the time so you can arrive on time and leave on time.

6. Telling the time is very important because then you can catch the right train.

7. I've learned that time is measured in twenty-four hours . . .

8. . . . and sixty minutes and sixty seconds.

9. I now know that "a.m." means morning and "p.m." means afternoon. So 2 a.m. would be 2 o'clock in the morning and 2 p.m. would be 2 o'clock in the afternoon.

Once we'd gathered in all of these ideas, I asked my students to group their contributions into three different categories. Though some of their responses could have been placed in two or even all three categories, Figure 2 shows what we decided was the main category for each one.

▶ Figure 2: Categorizing Student Responses

Understandings and Explanations	Judgments and Opinions	Comparisons and Connections
7. I've learned that time is measured in twenty-four hours . . . 8. . . . and sixty minutes and sixty seconds. 9. I know that "a.m." means morning and . . .	1. I was getting annoyed because . . . 2. I now understand how to tell the time with . . . 3. Telling the time is important because . . .	4. Telling the time is an important part of math. 5. When you start working, you will need to be able to tell the time . . . 6. Telling the time is very important because then you can catch the right train.

3.3 • ENCOURAGING AND ENGAGING

Getting your students to group their ideas is one way to show respect for their ideas. It also gives the opportunity to "air" their ideas so that others have the chance to question or support them.

Another way to respond is to use follow-up comments such as these to encourage and engage:

- Can anyone help John out with this question?
- How does that compare with what Sarah said?
- I'll explain that part again. Tell me if your understanding fits with my explanation.
- That is a judgment on your part. I'd like to hear your reasons.
- Does what you say apply in all cases?
- So what you think is "x is. . . . " Is that right?

The last example needs further explanation, for it is one of the most useful interventions you can make. It can take one of two forms:

- a **restatement** or repetition of the words used by a student
- a **reformulation** or paraphrase of the words used by a student

3.4 • RESTATING

Simply restate the words a student actually used, or use them in phrases like "So what you are saying is x, is that right?" or "Are you saying x?"

When you summarize, make sure you ask students whether your summary is accurate. As you do this, you will show that you believe what they have said is important. It will also give your students time to reflect on their statement and think, "Did I really say that? Did I mean to say that? Is that right?"

Restatement will also invite students to extend or qualify their original statements. Furthermore, by repeating or summarizing you will signal to everyone else in the group that it is important to listen to each other and to check for meaning before continuing.

Finally, restatement is a focusing strategy. It picks some statements from the sometimes confusing flow of talk and enables them to be considered systematically. And, of course, your students can also join in by restating the ideas of their peers as well as offering their own ideas and understandings.

Examples of Restatement

In the following example, a teacher is talking with some eight-year-olds about odd and even numbers. This extract shows how the dominant Initiate-Response-Evaluate (IRE) structure (see Section 2.0) can be opened up by *restatement* in order to make the students think for themselves and help each other understand the content better. The restatements are underlined.

Teacher: So is twelve an even or an odd number?

Student A: An odd number.

Teacher: An odd number, right?

Student A: Yes. Three fours are twelve.

Teacher: So you can divide twelve by three. Does that mean it is an odd number?

Student B: Twelve is an even number because we said yesterday that you can divide an even number by two.

Student A: Oh . . . yeah, that's what I mean.

Teacher: So student B says twelve can be divided by two. Is that right?

Student A: Yes.

Teacher: So you say it's an odd number, right?

Student A: It's an even number.

Teacher: Are you sure?

Student A: Yes.

Teacher: Why?

Student A: Because it can be divided by two.

Teacher: Is there only one rule?

Student A: Yes.

In the following example, a different teacher is talking with a group of fifteen-year-olds about a novel. Her simple repetition with the addition of "all" for clarification prompts a pupil to reconsider her statement. After she says, "Go on," the pupil expands on the similarities and differences between the female characters.

Girl: The female characters in this book are very timid. They don't stand up for themselves.

Teacher: You are saying that all the female characters are timid.

Girl: Well, most of them.

Teacher: Which ones do you think aren't timid?

Girl: Sarah . . . she has ambitions.

Teacher: Go on.

3.5 • REFORMULATING

It is often assumed that students have the language resources necessary to get the most out of dialogue or that they will acquire them at their own pace without systematic support. However, several simple strategies can deepen dialogue and accelerate children's ability to use the abstract language of reasoning explained here.

Educationalist Joan Tough (1977, p. 215) has a good way of putting this in her book *Talking and Learning*: "In dialogue, each participant must project into the other's meanings, trying, as it were, to judge the possibilities for meaning that the speaker has left unrecognized. . . . We look for the possibilities of meaning for the child in any particular context and help him to extend the interpretation he is making of it."

> Another way to engage people in dialogue is to reformulate what they say (e.g., So I guess what you are saying means that . . .).

Examples of Reformulation

In the following excerpt, a teacher asks a group of six-year-olds about what is important and unimportant to them. One boy says that shoelaces are important. Here, the concept of abilities introduced by the teacher becomes a tool for *all* the children to think with because it gathers common experiences (being aware of things you can and can't do) and provides a name (*abilities*). It enables the dialogue to move from a particular concern to a more general one.

The reformulation is underlined.

Teacher: What is important to you?

Boy: Shoelaces.

Teacher: Shoelaces are important to you?

Boy: Yes.

Teacher: Why is that?

Boy: Because I can't tie mine.

Teacher: Ah, <u>so things we can and can't do are important</u>. Is that right?

Boy: Yes, but I'll be able to tie them when I'm seven.

Teacher: I'm sure you will. (*to all the children*) What other abilities that you don't have now do you think you will have when you get older?

In this next example, some fourteen-year-olds talk about whether there could be a "just war." A boy reformulates a girl's initial statement but adds his own question based on her choice of words: "defending their country."

When reformulation becomes a familiar strategy, the students themselves will start to use the strategy because they are aware of how useful it is.

Girl: I think that whoever starts a war . . . it's their fault. But the people who retaliate would be partly guilty as well if they just heard that another country was going to attack them and beat them to it. But if they waited for the other country to attack them, then they are not guilty. They are just defending their country.

Boy: You said that if you attack them before they attack you, but you know they are going to attack you, that they are guilty because they fired the first shot. But aren't you still defending your country if you get in there first? You have the information that they are going to attack you.

Girl: No, because even though somebody might have told you that, you still don't know they are definitely going to do it and you could be jumping to conclusions. And you could start a war from nothing but rumours.

3.6 • REVIEW

This chapter has covered the following main points:

1. The most important standpoint for initiating fruitful dialogue is intellectual encouragement.

2. Intellectual encouragement includes listening, questioning and giving feedback to students.

3. A productive way to begin a dialogue is to ask your students to come up with questions or statements about the topic they are currently studying.

4. When responding to students' first ideas, it is useful to offer a restatement or reformulation of what they have said.

5. A restatement repeats the words spoken by a student back to them so as to check for meaning and/or intention.

6. A reformulation is paraphrasing what they have said, again to check for meaning, intention and/or consequence.

3.7 • NEXT STEPS AND FURTHER READING

Here are some suggestions to help you with your reflections on dialogue:

1. In what ways will you communicate an attitude of intellectual encouragement to your students?

2. As you plan your students' learning for the next week, identify times when you can issue invitations of the kind suggested in Section 3.2. Try to identify at least three different curriculum areas in which to use these invitations.

3. In the dialogues you have with students, make frequent use of the strategies of restatement and reformulation. Note the results.

4. Use some of the strategies mentioned in Chapters 8, 9 and 10.

5. Add the strategies from this section to the Repertoire and Judgment Notes at the back of this book.

To learn more about making conversation more dialogic, we recommend reading any of the following texts available online:

1. *Opening Dialogue: Understanding the Dynamics of Language and Learning in the English Classroom* (Nystrand, 1996)

   Martin Nystrand has researched classroom dialogue extensively. In this chapter he makes a clear distinction between what he calls "recitation" (the IRE structure mentioned in Section 2.0) and "dialogic exchange." He stresses the benefits of dialogic exchange in a way that supports the emphasis of this chapter on issuing invitations to students for dialogue.

   The first chapter of this book is available online at http://bit.ly/1AYgx6y.

2. **When Is Dialogue "Dialogic"?** (O'Connor & Michaels, 2007)

   The tactics of restatement and reformulation proposed in this chapter are based partly on the concept of voicing put forward by Catherine O'Connor and Sarah Michaels in this article. They are two of the primary researchers into revoicing and its benefits (see, e.g., Aligning Academic Task and Participation Status Through Revoicing: Analysis of a Classroom Discourse Strategy, *Anthropology and Education Quarterly, 24,* 318–335).

   Available online at http://bit.ly/1wZPkF7.

3. *Using Discussion in Classrooms* (Dillon, 1994)

   James T. Dillon is an authority on discussion and questioning. This book has a very useful collection (pp. 79–91) of moves to help discussions engage pupils. "Reflective restatement" is one of them and is a variation on restating and revoicing: "State your understanding of what the speaker has just said, giving your sense of it in one economical and exact sentence" (p. 81). Dillon's doubts about questioning as a strategy for pupil engagement are thought-provoking. His section on reflective restatement starts at page 31. This book is currently out of print, but a booklet by Dillon, *Teaching and the Art of Questioning,* is available online at the Education Resources Information Centre (ERIC): http://files.eric.ed.gov/fulltext/ED235133.pdf.

> "Reasons are the pillars of the mind."
>
> (Edward Albert Counsel, celebrated Tasmanian and Fellow of the Royal Geographical Society, 1849–1939)

ONE WAY TO LEARN *HOW* TO THINK
DEVELOP REASONING

This chapter was written by Steve Williams.

4.0 • PREVIEW

In the previous chapter we noted that although students will develop language as they grow, we should also provide systematic support to increase the quality and quantity of that language. In this chapter, we share some vocabulary that should help to provide that systematic support.

We also shared in Section 1.0 some of the conclusions from Robin Alexander's work. Quite rightly, he is keen that teachers should help students "build on" the ideas of others rather than simply exchange ideas with each other. It is, after all, through such building that the thinking and understanding of learning can be developed.

That said, Alexander provides no concrete suggestions as to how to build such dialogue. Instead, he just makes some general comments about the importance of asking appropriate questions. So in this chapter, we give you two frameworks that you can use to do exactly that: to build and deepen dialogue with your students.

> The language of reasoning is crucial for thinking, dialogue and writing of any complexity. The reasoning cards on the next couple of pages can help students develop their language of reasoning.

The language of reasoning is crucial for thinking, dialogue and writing of any complexity. Knowledge of the vocabulary that underpins reasoning will help your students understand, explore and make judgments in dialogue with others.

Over the next couple of pages is a selection of the most important of these expressions organized under four headings related to the kind of work they do. Some expressions appear under more than one heading.

Perhaps you could display these on your classroom walls for easy reference by your students. Alternatively, print them as cards for your students to use during collaborative group work. Remember that, as with all the resources in this book, full-color versions are available to download from www.challenginglearning.com.

The English educationalist, philosopher and literary critic Ivor Armstrong Richards suggested that words like those shown on the cards in Figure 3 are among the most "resourceful" in language because they help people think about everything else. In a striking sentence, Richards (1955, p. 10) says, "The senses of these chief words—and their ways of working with and against one another—are the rules of reason."

▶ Figure 3: Language of Reasoning Cards

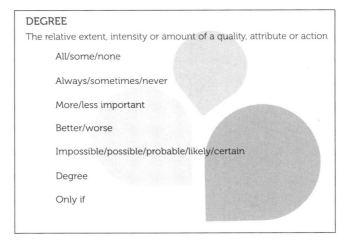

DEGREE
The relative extent, intensity or amount of a quality, attribute or action

All/some/none

Always/sometimes/never

More/less important

Better/worse

Impossible/possible/probable/likely/certain

Degree

Only if

DISCOURSE
The process of reasoning within a dialogue or writing

Question/answer

Statement/proposition/opinion

Hypothesis/premise/argument

Assumption/presupposition

If ... then

Unless

Agree/disagree

Reason/grounds

Principle/maxim

Evidence

Conclusion

Consequence

```
KIND
A classification distinguished by common essential characteristics

Question/attribute                      Is/are

Criterion                               Part/whole

All/some/none                           Example

Is/isn't                                Alternative

If ... then                             Addition

Group/class                             Kind
```

```
RELATION
The existence or effect of a connection or contrast between things

Cause/effect/consequence                Best/worst

Before/after/at the same time           If ... then

Same/similar/different/opposite         Part/whole

Certain/possible/probable/impossible    Means/end/purpose

Important/significant                   Connection/relation
```

4.2 • DEVELOPING THE LANGUAGE OF REASONING

If students are to think for themselves, then the language of reasoning should be developed deliberately and regularly in dialogue and in writing.

Below are two example dialogues. We have underlined the words particularly associated with the language of reasoning, both in the dialogues and in the commentary below each one.

In the first dialogue, the reasoning words serve two purposes: they allow the people engaged in the dialogue to make their arguments, and they help them reflect on the type of argument they are making.

> Dialogue can help students become more reasonable. It can also help them be more willing and able to learn.

Example 1

John: I think stem cell research should not be allowed because we shouldn't mess with human life. It's a principle. We shouldn't play at being God.

Sarah: I <u>disagree</u>. Stem cell research could help people with serious illnesses to live a <u>better</u> life. Maybe we shouldn't try to do it just because we can, or for cosmetic uses, but <u>only</u> to cure serious illnesses.

The underlined words are examples of terms that can be used to develop students' reasoning.

In order to progress further with this argument, John and Sarah would have to recognize that *principles* and *consequences* are involved. They would need to share background information and relate it to their *reasons*. Sarah might present more information about various treatments. John would consider whether to modify his <u>principle</u> into "You shouldn't mess with human life <u>unless</u> . . ."

They might <u>agree</u>, at least, that they both valued human life. Sarah might say, "People mess with human life all the time—people have operations. Why is stem cell research different in <u>principle</u> from that?"

The *language of reasoning* words we've underlined have two uses: to help John and Sarah make the arguments and to help them reflect on the arguments together. The words are tools, as are the moves of agreeing and comparing.

However, this tool metaphor only goes so far. They are more than tools: they are constituents of the people we have become.

Students become reasonable when they are able to use the language of reasoning to maintain control of their thoughts, when they understand how resourceful that language can be and when they are disposed to reason with others.

And if students can become more reasonable, they will bring their reasoning selves to lessons in all subjects—willing and able to learn better and understand more. All of this can be achieved through dialogue.

Example 2

The language of reasoning is often used to enable the constant adjustment and refining of thought that is distinctive of dialogue.

The following is an extract from *Student-Centered Language Arts and Reading* by Moffett and Wagner (1976). Again, we have underlined the reasoning words in the text.

Suppose the topic is "getting along in families." Opinions are piling up on all sides, but no idea is fastened and examined for a moment. Students are agreeing and disagreeing too quickly without knowing what the statements of others imply. They are lining up sides, identifying with or opposing other students. Word meanings are loose and unqualified. You suggest they linger over one statement:

The underlined words are examples of terms that can be used to develop students' reasoning.

Elle just said: "Younger children of a family get their own way more often than the older children." From what Bill just said it is clear that he disagrees. But look at her statement for a moment. Is it <u>never</u> true? Is it <u>always</u>? Instead of just accepting or rejecting it, see to what extent you can accept it and to what extent you cannot. In other words suggest a strategy of amending a statement until it becomes acceptable—that is, by qualifying and quantifying it. In regard to how many people is the statement true—<u>all</u>, <u>most</u>, <u>some</u>, a <u>few</u>? Can you offer examples and counterexamples? (Moffett & Wagner, 1976, p. 359)

4. One Way to Learn *How* to Think

4.3 • PROCESS OF REASONING

Figure 4 shows some of the reasoning cards that you can print and give to your students. The full set is available online at www.challenginglearning.com. We suggest you distribute the full set to your students, making sure each student gets one card, the next time you run a dialogue with them.

Students need to learn how to use the language of reasoning. The process of reasoning cards on the next few pages can be displayed or given to students to support their reasoning skills.

▶ Figure 4: **Process of Reasoning Cards**

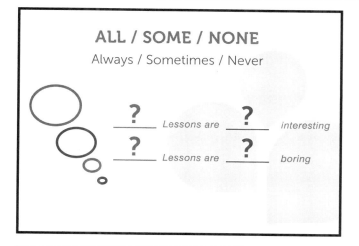

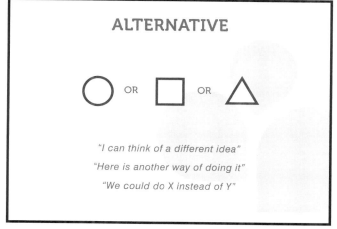

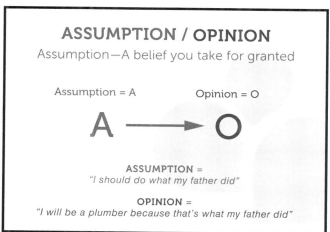

CONSEQUENCE
CAUSE . . . EFFECT / IF . . . THEN

"If I did that then . . ."

"If that was true then . . ."

"That happened because . . ."

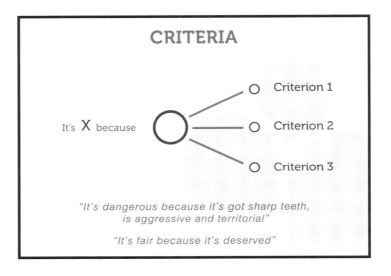

CRITERIA

It's **X** because

Criterion 1

Criterion 2

Criterion 3

*"It's dangerous because it's got sharp teeth,
is aggressive and territorial"*

"It's fair because it's deserved"

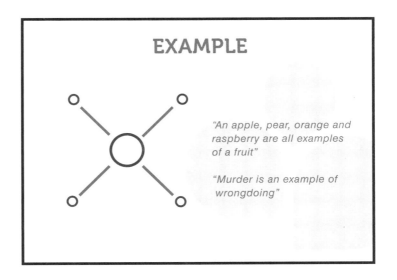

EXAMPLE

*"An apple, pear, orange and
raspberry are all examples
of a fruit"*

*"Murder is an example of
wrongdoing"*

IMPOSSIBLE / POSSIBLE / LIKELY / CERTAIN

✗	✗	✗	*Impossible*	*No way!*
✗	✓	✗	*Possible*	*Maybe!*
✓	✓	✗	*Likely*	*Probably!*
✓	✓	✓	*Certain*	*Definitely!*

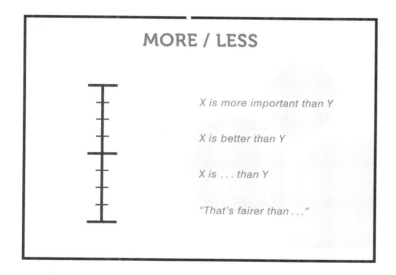

MORE / LESS

X is more important than Y

X is better than Y

X is ... than Y

"That's fairer than ..."

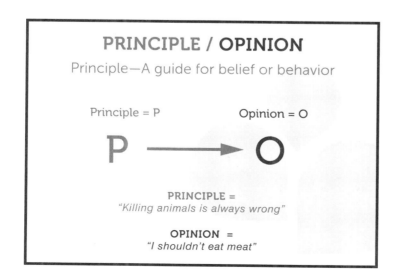

PRINCIPLE / OPINION

Principle—A guide for belief or behavior

Principle = P   Opinion = O

P ⟶ O

PRINCIPLE =
"Killing animals is always wrong"

OPINION =
"I shouldn't eat meat"

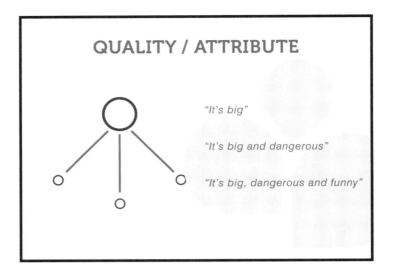

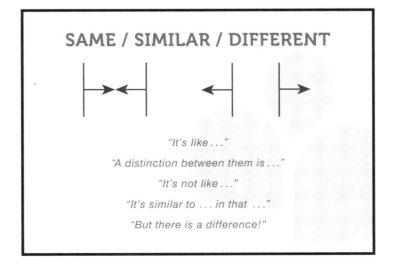

4. One Way to Learn *How* to Think

Using the Process of Reasoning Cards

Before you begin the next dialogue with your students, give them each one of the reasoning cards. Ask them to read the card they've got and then to talk in pairs about what they think their card is inviting them to do.

Then begin the dialogue with your students by issuing invitations (see Section 3.2). As the dialogue progresses, ask each student to listen for when their reasoning move could be made.

For example, if student A has the Assumption/Opinion card, then he will be listening for another student giving an opinion based on an assumption. For example, one student states the opinion:

- I think we should play more sports at school.

The student holding the Assumption/Opinion card might intervene in the dialogue at this point to ask what the assumption is that the opinion is based on. For example:

- Are you saying we should do more sports because you assume sports are a good thing to do?

- Or perhaps because sports promote healthy lifestyles?

- Or is your assumption that everyone, like you, enjoys sports?

Here are some other ways to use the cards:

1. Pause the dialogue and ask all students to identify examples of when their reasoning move was—or could have been—used.

2. Challenge each student to use their reasoning move at least once during the dialogue.

3. Display all the cards on your classroom walls so that your students can refer to them whenever they are engaging in dialogue.

4. Set up a system of Dialogue Detectives (see Section 5.4 A and Chapter 6). Give the cards to the detectives, and get them to record the instances of their reasoning move being used. And/or get them to hold up their card at the point at which they think their reasoning move is being made or could be made.

5. Talk with your students about each and every card, explaining how the moves can be made, how they link with other moves and how they can be applied in different areas of the curriculum.

6. A more advanced activity would be to get small groups to structure their dialogues according to the next reasoning move they think should be made. For example, if someone offers *alternatives*, that move ought to lead to the possible *consequences* of those alternatives being imagined. That, in turn, should lead to a move of ranking the consequences by considering which ones would be the *most* and *least* desirable. And this would depend on establishing *criteria* for judging an item as being more or less desirable.

As your students become more familiar with these moves, they will learn about the significant difference between conversation and dialogue. They will also begin to understand the patterns of moves that make inquiry both possible and rewarding.

> Some of the best ways to use the process of reasoning cards include splitting them up between different groups, making one card the focus for a dialogue and teaching each process in turn over a series of lessons.

4.4 • ROUTINES TO DEVELOP REASONING

Ways to develop students' thinking skills include drawing attention to the language of reasoning, using reasoning terms systematically and pausing for writing breaks to record the most effective terms used.

Here are some more ideas for helping your students appropriate the language of reasoning:

1. Stress the language of reasoning in all the dialogues you have with students. Use the language yourself by reformulating students' contributions to include important terms from the cards shown in Figure 3.

   So if one student says, "I've got another idea," ask if they think it is a different idea from those raised so far and, if so, in what ways.

   If someone says, "X happens because of Y," you might say, "So is X a <u>consequence</u> of Y?"

   Follow that up with "What are some of the other <u>possible consequences</u>?" and "Which <u>consequences</u> do you think are <u>most important</u>?"

2. Show students how they can inquire systematically into an issue using a succession of questions that incorporate key expressions from the language of reasoning. Show them how you put a series of questions together.

   For example, prompt students by asking, "What questions do you have at this point?" or "What do you think your next three questions about this will be?"

   Draw their attention to the usefulness of the terms given in Figure 3 for framing questions such as "What are the alternatives?" "What is similar and different about them?" "What would the consequences be if one of those alternatives were chosen?"

3. Help students use diagrams and written lists when reasons, examples, similarities or causes need to be gathered and analyzed. Diagrams and lists will focus joint attention.

4. Use writing breaks during a dialogue for students to record and develop their thoughts. Give them prompts taken from the list given in Figure 3, such as these:

   Write at least four *examples* of . . .

   What are some of the *criteria* for . . . ?

   Then restart the dialogue incorporating the ideas gathered by the writing.

5. Focus from time to time on one term from the language of reasoning cards (or another you think important) and create an activity to help students become more familiar with the part it plays in reasoning. We provide some examples in the next chapter.

4.5 • DEVELOPING A REASONING REPERTOIRE

Drawing attention to the ways reasoning can be used in any given context will build students' dialogue skills.

Forgive the rather clichéd analogy, but just as cabin crew on an airplane say to put on your own mask before helping others, so it is with almost everything we aim to teach our students: we should develop our own skills before helping others. This section shows some ways you can develop your own reasoning repertoire before helping others.

Contextualize

Don't be too general. Instead of always using the same general phrase in all situations, such as "What are your assumptions?" be more specific and sensitive to the context.

For example, if a student says, "You will live longer if you give up eating meat," then you might respond, "Are you assuming that *all* vegetarians are healthy?" Once you get an answer to that, ask other students to identify the assumptions being made. Move away from the general questions that can be used in all situations (e.g., What are your assumptions? Can you give me some examples?). Instead, listen to what the students say, and gauge your responses to the particulars of the conversation.

Use Reasoning Terms Deliberately

When students say things that imply certain language-of-reasoning moves (see Figure 3), draw attention to the terms that might be used. For example, if someone says, "Not all vegetarians are healthy," you could say, "Yes, people might assume that vegetarians are healthy. But might there be reasons why some vegetarians are not healthy?" By reinforcing these terms and showing when they could be used, you will help everyone in the dialogue understand what is going on and how meaning and opinion are being created and questioned.

Use Encouragement as Well as Questions

Don't always ask questions. Sometimes just say things such as, "That's interesting. Tell me what you think the alternatives are." By doing this, you are indicating what you think the next move in the dialogue should be.

4.6 • REASONING MOVES

Reasoning moves provide a structure for thinking together. Here are some examples that should help you develop your repertoire for reasoning:

1. Understand Something

A: To understand something, we should know how it is similar to and different from other things.

Move: Ask for similarities and differences.

Examples: How is a volcano different from a mountain? Are courage and bravery the same thing? What are the differences and similarities between an empire and a colony?

Follow-ups: Which similarities and differences are most significant? Which are based on fact and which on opinion?

B: To understand something, we should know how it fits into a system.

Move: Ask if something is part of a system or part of a bigger whole or part of a common pattern.

Examples: Atoms are parts of molecules, right? So what is the relationship between them? What part do rivers play in settlement? What part does challenge play in achievement?

Follow-ups: Does this have an effect on something else (is it a cause of something)? Is this an effect of something else? Is this always/usually a part of something?

C: To understand something, we should know the effects that it has or that it might have under certain conditions.

> Reasoning moves are deliberate actions a participant can make to ensure a dialogue is more exploratory.

> Understanding something better includes knowing how it compares to something else . . .

> . . . knowing how it fits into the bigger picture . . .

Move: Ask what the effects of something are (or might be).

Examples: Why are water and sunlight important for seeds? What effects does sunlight have on seeds? If we put seeds in soil and leave them in a dark room, what would the consequence be? What are the effects of deforestation?

Follow-ups: What are the most important effects of deforestation? What makes an effect important? Is it to do with who is affected by it? Are animal and plant life as important as human life? What is the difference between the words *effect* and *affect*? Are they connected?

D: To understand something, we should recognize its significance and importance.

Move: Ask why something is important/significant.

Examples: What is important about our heart? Is it as important as our bones? Is it as important as our skeleton? Is it the same for other animals? Who is the most important character in this story? What is the most significant moment in this story?

Follow-ups: What reasons do you have for your choices? Are things important only because of their consequences, or are there other reasons?

2. Evaluate Something

E: To evaluate something, we should be aware of criteria.

Move: When someone has offered an evaluation or is about to make one, ask what criteria he or she is using or ask what possible criteria are appropriate for that evaluation.

Examples: If students say a piece of writing is "good," ask, "What makes it good?" If they say, for example, "It is very vivid," you could say, "So vividness is one criterion for good writing. What other criteria might there be?"

Different products and activities have different criteria that students should become familiar with. Having this kind of exploratory dialogue will help.

Follow-ups: You could keep going to deeper levels. "Good" writing is the most general level; "vivid" writing is less general but you could ask, "What are your criteria for vividness?" or "What makes a piece of writing vivid?" Go as deep as you think appropriate. You could also ask for alternatives and say, "What are other possible criteria for this kind of writing (or inquiry or action or performance or artwork or design)?" You might also explore relative importance: "What criteria are most important for this kind of thing, or are they all as important as each other?"

F: To evaluate something we should consider consequences/effects.

Move: This is linked with the previous item on criteria. One kind of criterion for evaluating is to take into account the consequences/effects of an action or choice and set those against the consequences of alternative actions or choices.

Examples: The writer uses the word *mob*. What effect does that have on the reader? What if the writer had used a more neutral word like *group*? In a history lesson, someone might express the view that a particular invasion or other act was a "mistake." It would be important to ask whether this judgment is based on a principle (e.g., all invasions are wrong) or a consequence (e.g., bad things happened because of the invasion).

Follow-ups: Taking the example of the invasion, if the judgment is based on a consequence, you might ask for criteria on a deeper level: "What made those consequences bad?" You might also use an if/then move: "If there was no invasion, then what might have happened next?" When you get some responses to this counterfactual question, you might make the move to ask whether the imagined consequences were possible, probable or highly likely.

3. Generalize

Principle and move: You should be aware when you are generalizing, then test the generalization by deliberately searching for exceptions (counter-examples) and assessing their significance.

Examples: If someone says, "Snakes are poisonous," ask, "Are you saying all snakes are poisonous?" If the answer is yes, the next move might be "Is that right?" or "Can anyone think of any non-poisonous snakes?" Once you have counter-examples or if the original answer is no, the next move you could make is to seek more precision: "So are most snakes poisonous or just a few?"

Follow-ups: You could return to assess the generalization: "Is this generalization wrong?" You could also go for deeper understanding: "Do the poisonous snakes have anything else in common?" or "Why are some snakes poisonous and some not?" (e.g., looking at factors like arid environments and types of prey). If the generalization is an evaluation (e.g., "all invasions are bad"), then the next move could be to ask for criteria for "bad" (see the item above on criteria).

> Testing something's general principles should include a search for possible exceptions.

4.7 • REVIEW

This chapter has covered the following main points:

1. Students should learn to build on the ideas of others rather than simply exchange ideas with each other.

2. The language of reasoning is crucial for thinking, dialogue and writing of any complexity.

3. Knowledge of the vocabulary that underpins reasoning will help your students understand, explore and make judgments in dialogue with others.

4. The most important expressions of reasoning can be divided into four categories: To what *degree* is that statement correct? What *kind* of reason is that? What *relation* does that idea have to another? What are some of the general moves of *discourse* that one might make?

5. Students become reasonable when they are able to use the language of reasoning to maintain control of their thoughts, when they understand how resourceful that language can be and when they are disposed to reason with others.

6. The language of reasoning can be used to enable the constant adjustment and refining of thought within a dialogue.

4.8 • NEXT STEPS

Here are some suggestions for what you could do next so that you get the most out of this chapter:

1. Read the language of reasoning terms (Figure 3 in Section 4.1), and choose which ones to share with your students.

2. Print out the process of reasoning cards (Figure 4 in Section 4.3), or download them from www.challenginglearning.com.

3. Choose which cards you are going to share with your students. Explain each one in turn and encourage students to use the cards during the next dialogue.

4. Reflect on the effect of these actions, and choose which ones to use next.

5. Use at least two of the strategies suggested in Section 4.4.

6. Try out some of the scenarios in Section 4.6 to increase your reasoning repertoire.

7. Add the strategies you've found most useful to your notes in the Repertoire and Judgment Notes section at the back of this book.

> "Human activity consists of action and reflection: it is praxis; it is transformation of the world. And as praxis, it requires theory to illuminate it. Human activity and practice; it is reflection and action."
>
> (Friere, 2001)

DIALOGUE GROUPINGS

5.0 • PREVIEW

This chapter is about the differences between whole-group and small-group arrangements. In it, we suggest strategies for making each of them effective. In particular, we

- introduce Dialogue Detectives and panel dialogues,
- stress the importance of ground rules for dialogue,
- provide a sequence for small-group dialogue.

Neither small-group nor whole-group dialogue works best for every situation. It is important to develop judgment about what is the most appropriate dialogue structure for each learning activity that you plan.

> There are many ways to group students for dialogue. This chapter explores some of the best approaches.

5.1 • DIALOGUE GROUPINGS

The strategies for dialogue we have given so far have not stipulated group size. They could be used with whole-class groups or with a small group when the teacher is present.

The situation will change if you are working with other students while a particular group is running its own small-group dialogue. So in this chapter we show you what you can do, so that dialogue will work with a range of groupings.

First, however, it is important to stress the relevance to all types of groupings of the strategies offered in the previous chapters:

Issuing Invitations

The nature of the invitation matters! Whatever the size of group, the quality of the dialogue will depend on the quality and appropriateness of the invitation to think.

> **Students should have something to gain from having a dialogue, whether it is better understandings of issues, better solutions to problems or better answers to questions of judgment.**

Encouraging Students to Think

As mentioned in Chapter 3, your stance of intellectual encouragement toward students is also important. Remember, you are working to create a classroom community of thinkers who can tackle questions together and work toward the best answers and understandings. You should demonstrate to students your belief that they can become that community. Therefore, your invitations should be challenging *and* supportive. Your students should know what is expected of them.

Using Dialogue "Moves" and the Language of Reasoning

As discussed in Chapter 4, the language your students use during a dialogue will very much decide how clear, coherent and comprehensive the outcomes are. So the more your students know when and how to articulate the following (as examples), the more their dialogue will be focused and clear:

- Give reasons.
- Ask for examples.
- Suggest alternatives.
- Restate.
- Reformulate.

There are, of course, many other moves your students can make, as shown in Chapter 4. The more your students take part in structured dialogue, the more you model, prompt and explain these moves, the more proficient your students will become.

5.2 • GROUND RULES FOR DIALOGUE GROUPS

Observation by researchers of small-group talk often reveals that much of the talk that goes on in classrooms is not educationally productive or helpful for extending students' skills and understandings. It seems that many students do not use talk to work well together—and perhaps do not know how to do so.

Researchers have found that an important way for teachers to provide support is to ask students to decide on what they consider to be "the six most important rules that people talking in groups should follow" (Wegerif, 2002, pp. 3–4).

Here are the rules recommended by Wegerif (2002):

Our Talking Rules

- We share our ideas and listen to each other.

- We talk one at a time.

- We respect each other's opinions.

- We give reasons to explain our ideas.

- If we disagree we ask "why?"

- We try to agree in the end if we can.

These rules are not set in stone! You do not have to use these rules. Indeed, it might be better to create a set of rules with your students (see Section 2.6.4). That way, they will have a sense of ownership and will more likely understand the meanings fully.

Whichever way you decide to go—presenting the list above or creating a new list with your students—you should ensure there is an opportunity for your students to talk about the meanings of the rules and to agree on the precise wording of the rules.

Once this is complete, make sure the ground rules are displayed prominently for easy reference and reminding. This might seem unnecessary. Yet researchers have found that a simple set of agreed-upon ground rules that are constantly referred to have a far greater influence on improving the quality and focus of dialogues than rules that are established but not frequently referred to. This is particularly true when students are working in smaller collaborative groups.

> Establishing clear ground rules will significantly increase the effectiveness of small-group dialogues.

5.3 • WHOLE-GROUP DIALOGUE

Whole-group dialogue covers a wide range of situations. A dialogue could arise out of the general flow of a lesson, For example, we might think that the talk among our students is rather lacking direction or cohesion, or we might decide that greater understanding, exploration or judgment is required. In this case, we can modulate the talk into dialogue by issuing an invitation to students (see Section 3.2) or simply restating or reformulating a student's response (see Sections 3.4 and 3.5).

For example:

- "Let's consider Emilia's question for a moment."

- "That's interesting, John. I think that would be worth talking more about. What do other people think about what John said?"

- "You say an extinct volcano will never erupt again, is that right?"

On the other hand, whole-group dialogue can be a planned event. As you plan your lessons, you might decide that the learning will be best served via a whole-group dialogue. If this is the case, then it is a good idea to prepare your invitation carefully so that the dialogue can begin with a well-chosen question or series of questions.

Small-group dialogues are a better choice when students need to carry out an activity prior to answering a question; for example, they might sift information, imagine possibilities and consequences, collect examples or conduct experiments.

> The dividing line between whole-group and small-group dialogue is blurred. Even in a whole-group dialogue you are likely to pause, have students talk in pairs or small groups and then return to the main question.

For example, you might say:

- "Talk in pairs about your first thoughts on this question."
- "Get into groups of three. Be sure to include anyone who is left out. Collect all the examples of (for example, unfairness) you can think of, and try to group them according to kinds of unfairness."
- "We've been discussing the question 'What makes a good math problem?'" People have suggested some criteria. Now we are going to work in groups to create a math problem for other groups to solve."

Benefits of Whole-Group Dialogues

> When everyone focuses on the same question, there is maximum opportunity for students to learn from each other as well as from you. This includes learning dialogue moves and essential language that you are modeling.

There will often be a "community feel" to the dialogue, particularly if you promote the culture of inquiry mentioned in Section 3.1.

Since you will all be sharing the same dialogue space, you should be able to support, challenge and encourage your students more effectively.

There is no need for time-consuming report-backs because everyone is involved in the same dialogue at the same time.

Drawbacks of Whole-Group Dialogues

Speaking in front of a large group can intimidate some students.

If you are not careful, unhelpful patterns can emerge. For example, some students might dominate the dialogue, whereas others might not speak at all, whatever their level of interest in the topic.

Even when everyone is interested, there often isn't enough time or opportunity for everyone to contribute, which can lead to some students withdrawing mentally from the dialogue.

What Works for You?

In the Introduction we stressed the need to develop good judgment alongside the increasing repertoire of strategies that this book offers you. Many problems of whole-group dialogue can be overcome with the appropriate combination of useful strategies coupled with the good judgment arising from experience and from dialogue with colleagues.

5.4 • SPLITTING LARGE GROUPS INTO TWO

One way to make whole-group dialogues more manageable is to split your students into two groups. These don't necessarily need to be of equal size (see Chapter 6). One half can take part in the dialogue with you as normal while the other half can observe and make notes (or give verbal reflections if they are too young to write). Below are two models for this: Dialogue Detectives and panel dialogues. Please note that we describe Dialogue Detectives in more detail in Chapter 6.

A. Dialogue Detectives

This setup involves two concentric circles of students. Students in the inner circle engage in a dialogue while students in the outer circle observe and make notes. Those in the outer circle should focus on things they agree and disagree with or have further questions about. Alternatively, they can prepare feedback to give to the inner circle (for example, about the quality of the dialogue that took place and the group dynamics they observed). In this way, the students you place in the outer circle are detectives. They are looking for clues relating to high-quality dialogue—the moves being made, the reasons being given, the attentiveness of the listeners and so on.

Dialogue in the inner circle is carried on in the same way as it would be for the whole group, but students get more opportunity to speak and to receive feedback from their peers. The performance aspect might frighten some, but it will excite others.

At some point during the dialogue (perhaps every ten to fifteen minutes), the two groups of students can exchange places so that each one gets a chance of being in the inner circle for part of the time and being a Dialogue Detective at other times. This process repeats itself a few times over.

B. Panel Dialogues

Panel dialogues provide a useful means to limit the number of people who can speak at one time. They work very well, even with as many as sixty people at a time.

To set up a panel dialogue, divide your students into groups of about three or four. Get each group to discuss a question or statement for five to ten minutes. You can provide the starting question, or you can invite suggestions from the whole class before they get into smaller groups.

Choose one or two people from each group to come to the front of the room and take part in a dialogue. Sit them in a horseshoe arrangement (or as close to that as the space will allow) so that they can easily see each other as well as the audience.

You lead the dialogue. To give a sense of fairness, you could give each student a number within his or her group, then invite, for example, all the number threes to take part in the horseshoe dialogue. The rest of the class should observe and make notes, using some of the suggestions from the discussion of Dialogue Detectives in Chapter 6.

You can swap panel members over after a short time or let one panel talk for longer and then choose a different panel in another lesson when the issue changes.

You could make membership of the panel voluntary, then monitor who does and doesn't volunteer. Those who don't can be given some coaching and encouragement away from their peers. Those who dominate could be given a maximum limit for their panel appearances. It is up to you how you use this idea.

> Shifting between whole-group and small-group dialogues is generally the best way to teach good thinking habits while also increasing student participation.

> Dialogue Detectives is a great way to engage students during whole-class dialogues.

> Panel dialogues are another good way to increase motivation of students in a large group.

> **Panel dialogue is a useful and flexible variation on whole-class work that also incorporates some small-group dialogue. You can observe one or more of the small groups to see how students organize themselves and use the language of reasoning.**

You can also lead one of the groups that you think needs your extra support.

5.5 • SMALL-GROUP DIALOGUES WITH A TEACHER

In this arrangement, you work with one small group of up to six students while the rest of your students work on a task that can be completed independently.

> *Splitting students into small groups and then guiding each group in turn can be a very effective way to teach good thinking.*

Your role is similar to that in a whole-group discussion, but there is more opportunity for the students you are working with to speak and less chance they will be intimidated by speaking in front of lots of others.

You can also organize the best combination of students for particular groups to suit a particular purpose. For example:

- Having the same set of students for each dialogue may promote a sense of continuity and familiarity to support risk taking and the uninhibited sharing of ideas.

- Mixing up students might help them work with other people to promote class cohesion and understanding.

- Grouping with consideration for ability, gender and levels of extroversion will also have an impact on dialogue.

Observing Rather Than Leading

> *Be careful about the pros and cons of dividing students in different ways.*

Small-group dialogues with you simply watching rather than leading can also provide good opportunities for observation and coaching.

For example, you could do one of the following:

- Tell the group they are going to discuss a question or complete a task themselves without your help. Observe the group's performance. This gives you a lot of information about their progress in conducting a dialogue, making appropriate moves and using the language of reasoning. Give feedback according to criteria you have established with them (see Chapter 6 and Appendix 1 for examples), and ask them to evaluate themselves.

- Observe for a while, and give students prompts or reminders of things they can do to improve the dialogue, such as asking others what they think or asking the whole group if anyone has alternative suggestions. Then let them continue and evaluate together at the end.

5.6 • SMALL-GROUP DIALOGUES WITHOUT A TEACHER

Very often it seems better to split large groups of students into lots of smaller groups. This of course means you won't be able to work with all the small groups at the same

time. So here is what you can do to maintain at least some sense of quality and direction:

1. Split your students into groups of three or four.

2. Establish clear ground rules (see Sections 2.6.4 and 5.2).

3. Get all groups to discuss a question or complete a task simultaneously.

4. Ensure that every group is very clear about the sequence of activities you have set up.

> **The orchestration of multiple groups is very important. Routines and sequences need to be clearly understood so the students will, to the maximum extent, be able to carry out the tasks themselves.**
>
> **Two vital areas to consider are establishing general ground rules for dialogue and developing a clear sequence of activities so your students know what to expect.**

A Sequence for Small-Group Work

There are many similar sequences offered in the literature on dialogue in small groups. We have chosen one that can be used with some of the activities offered later in this book, such as Mysteries, Odd One Out and Fortune Lines.

There are five stages:

1. **Setting the scene**

2. **Exploration**

3. **Main dialogue**

4. **Presentation**

5. **Reflection**

Setting up a clear sequence for small-group dialogues will increase the chances of success.

A. Setting the Scene

There is much more to do in preparation for small-group work than just giving out the materials and explaining the task.

- You should explain to your students why they are doing the task, how the task fits in with a particular unit of work and how it links to what they have done in the past.

- You can then present a question or problem in such a way as to intrigue your students and challenge them to engage with it.

- You should ensure that your students have sufficient background knowledge to tackle the question or challenge. If they don't already know the details, then give them a quick rundown of the basic information they will need to begin the task. (This is the surface-level knowledge they will need from which to build toward deeper understanding; see Section 1.2.)

- Finally, before they begin, draw attention to the ground rules of dialogue (see Sections 2.6.4 and 5.2) and discuss any other criteria for judging the dialogue and the outcome of the task. For example: Is it concise? Is it persuasive? Does it work?

B. Exploration

Encourage your students to think aloud in response to the task. This will give them the chance to clarify their initial thoughts to the group and to generate possible alternatives and supporting reasons. Allow a short amount of time for this exploration, during which you can monitor the groups to ensure they understand the task and prompt each other to contribute and generally stick to the agreed-upon ground rules.

C. Main Dialogue

After the scene is set and the initial exploration phase completed, your students can begin to engage in the main dialogue. To help them along the way, we recommend you use at least one of the strategies described in Chapters 8, 9 and 10.

> **The choice of the main activity is crucial to the quality of learning. Ideally, it will be challenging and open to a range of strategies, answers, solutions or conclusions.**

There are many examples at the back of this book as well as online for members of the Challenging Learning Process at www.challenginglearning.com.

D. Presentation

Ask your students to present their results to other groups. This will probably generate some excitement and energy as well as nervousness. The main purpose, though, is to enhance understanding—not just for the listeners but also for the presenters, since an effective way of learning something comes from explaining to others.

A good way to organize the presentation phase is to make a distinction between "home" and "away" groupings.

- **Home groups** are relatively stable groupings in which students work with the same classmates each time. These groups do not change between lessons, although they may be reviewed periodically.

- **Away groups** are more fluid than home groups and are created for just one activity. Sharing groups will vary in size according to the task. A sharing group could comprise only two students presenting to each other, or it could involve two or three students from each home group presenting to similar numbers from other groups, up to a limit of about nine in total.

- **A panel dialogue** (see Section 5.4 B) could also be used as a structure for sharing. Each panel would be a sharing group. The central point about a sharing group is that it enables different views and solutions to be heard so as to prompt comparison and reflection. Alternatively, the whole class can be a sharing group. If this is the case, one or two students from each home group are given the task of summarizing their group's conclusions.

E. Reflection

Reflection might come at any part of the sequence. It involves the whole group coming together to discuss things such as the following:

Bringing the groups together to make a presentation to each other can enhance understanding for presenters as well as listeners.

It is very important to finish any sequence of dialogues with shared reflections about effectiveness, conclusions drawn and methods used.

- **Conclusions**: What were the differences and similarities between the conclusions of the various groups? Were they significant? Why? Would anyone like to offer criteria for judging any of the outcomes as better or worse than others?

- **The Process**: Is everyone working well together in their groups? Are they following the ground rules? (See Sections 2.6.4 and 5.2.) Are they using the language of reasoning? (See Figure 3 in Section 4.1.)

- **Problems**: What are the main problems and questions so far? Is there anything we need to discuss now?

F. What's In It—For Me

Broadcasting on Radio Wii-FM

There is so much to be gained from dialogue. As we've discussed already, there are benefits in terms of learning to be reasonable, in deepening understanding and of increasing clarity. However, these gains might not be sufficient to inspire or motivate your students!

As we know, students value activities that give them an increased sense of control over their own thinking and their ability to influence the thinking of others.

Motivation is also related to the content. Unfortunately, when asked why they are discussing a question or deliberating on how to complete a task, students too often say, "Because we were told to." Frequently they see no purpose in a task beyond complying with instructions.

Therefore, picking up on the points made in Chapter 3, it is worth asking the following questions:

- Does the question or task I am designing relate to students' interests and/or priorities?

- Will it enhance their understanding of something important?

- Will it prompt them to reflect on significant things they would not have considered without the dialogue?

If we can answer yes to all three questions, then we maximize the chance of broadcasting on Radio Wii-FM (What's In It—For Me).

And remember, if your students ask, "Why are we doing this?" then it might actually be a genuine question!

> Motivate students by broadcasting on Radio Wii-FM (**W**hat's **I**n **I**t—**F**or **M**e).

5.7 • FINAL WORD ABOUT GROUPINGS

> **There is no one correct answer to the question "How shall I group students?" As always, it comes down to repertoire and judgment.**

According to Robert Marzano's meta-analyses of hundreds of studies examining the group options (Marzano, Pickering & Pollock, 2001):

1. Organizing students in cooperative learning groups has a powerful effect on learning (effect size = 0.78, the equivalent to doubling the rate of learning).

2. Cooperative groups should be kept to pairs or, at the most, groups of three or four.

3. Cooperative learning should be applied consistently and systematically but not overused. For example, one way to vary the grouping patterns would be to have:

   - informal groups (e.g., talk partners, turn to your neighbor and share a question/idea/connection),

   - formal groups that are set for the completion of a task over a number of days or weeks and include individual and group accountability,

   - base groups that stick together for a term or a year and complete a range of planned, informal and social tasks together.

Having said all that, we should also remind ourselves that collaborative groups are not always the best way forward. Sometimes the desire to achieve consensus and work together amiably can lead to a disregard of critical thinking. This is sometimes referred to as "groupthink."

Here are a few signs that cooperative groups might be sacrificing thoughtfulness for the sake of efficiency:

Overestimation of the group—members see themselves as infallible as well as superior to all other groups.

Intolerance—members tend to reject any outside views that do not fit with their own. They also create, or draw attention to, negative stereotypes of others.

Pressure to conform—within the team, there is a strong intolerance for differing opinions. Members with dissenting views are pressured to protect the status quo.

5.8 • REVIEW

In this chapter, we have explored the differences between whole-class and small-group arrangements and we have suggested strategies to make each of them effective.

Key points have included:

1. Neither small-group nor whole-group dialogue works best for every situation. It is important to develop judgment about what is the most appropriate structure for each occasion.

2. Researchers have found six important rules for group dialogue: share ideas and listen to others; talk one at a time; respect others' opinions; give reasons to explain ideas; when disagreeing, ask "why"; try to reach an agreement.

3. The main benefit of whole-group dialogues is that everyone can focus on the same question, with maximum opportunity for students to learn from each other as well as from you.

4. The main drawback of whole-group dialogue is there often isn't enough time or opportunity for everyone to contribute, leading to some students withdrawing mentally from the dialogue.

5. If you opt for multiple small groups, there are two vital aspects to consider: establishing general ground rules for dialogue and developing a clear sequence of activities so your students know what to expect.

6. When students work in small groups, there should be time for each group to present their strategies and conclusions to the whole class.

7. Cooperative groups should be kept to no more than three or four students per group.

5.9 • NEXT STEPS AND FURTHER READING

Here are some suggestions for what you could do next so that you get the most out of this chapter:

1. Try out a Dialogue Detectives session with your students (also see Chapter 6), and then reflect on the relative success of the approach (reflect with your students for the greatest impact).

2. Establish a set of ground rules in discussion with your students (see Sections 2.6.4 and 5.2). Display the rules in your classroom, and use them for whole-class and small-group work.

3. Use the sequence presented in Section 5.5 for small-group dialogues.

4. Add the strategies from this section to your Repertoire and Judgment Notes at the back of this book.

You could also read one or more of the following resources to deepen your understanding of dialogue groupings.

1. Neil Mercer, whose work we recommended in Chapter 2, provides a very useful summary of some of the differences between whole-class and small-group dialogue within an overall argument for dialogic teaching. See http://bit .ly/1MJ2VV6

2. The Dialogue Detectives arrangement for whole-class discussion was created based on the idea of the Socratic Circle. Copeland (2005) gives a good introduction to this convention in *Socratic Circles: Fostering Critical and Creative Thinking in Middle and High School.*

3. Another type of Socratic Circle comes from *The Paideia Proposal: An Educational Manifesto* (Adler, 1998). This involves getting students to ask questions of each other and engage in a dialogue about what they do and do not understand. The teacher must not get involved in the questions and answers. Instead, the teacher remains the facilitator of the interactions between students. One interesting reflection from James Hattie (2011, p. 215) goes as follows:

   The quality of the questions and the assertiveness of some answers scared me, as they clearly did not understand what I had so beautifully taught. I realized I had built the skill of asking questions about what I had just said and looking for the students (there are always some) who were keen to retell the story and to nod at the right times (to ensure I continued); they all knew the game we played. Of course, learning occurs when the students learn, not when the teacher has satisfactorily taught.

> "The most important thing in communication is to hear what isn't being said."
>
> (Drucker, 2007)

DIALOGUE DETECTIVES

6.0 • PREVIEW

This chapter is about Dialogue Detectives. Our former colleague Louise Brown created Learning Detectives as a way to help her young students learn how to give themselves and each other feedback. We have written about this in *Challenging Learning Through Feedback* (Nottingham & Nottingham, 2017) as part of this Challenging Learning series.

Inspired by Louise's idea, we have built on her approach to create Dialogue Detectives.

Dialogue Detectives look for clues relating to high-quality dialogue.

6.1 • APPOINTING DIALOGUE DETECTIVES

Dialogue Detectives are students who have been nominated to stay outside of the dialogue. Their job is to look for clues relating to high-quality dialogue.

The number of students appointed as Dialogue Detectives can range from just one or two to half the class.

If you are working with a relatively small group of students (e.g., fewer than twenty), then you might nominate only two or three students at a time to be Dialogue Detectives. Whereas if you have a large group, then you might split the students into two groups of equal number, with one group at any one time acting as the Dialogue Detectives.

Both setups involve two groups of students. Students in the main group engage in a dialogue; students outside the dialogue act as Dialogue Detectives. These detectives are looking for clues relating to high-quality dialogue, such as the reasoning "moves" (see Figure 4 in Section 4.3) being made, the reasons being given, the attentiveness of the listeners and so on.

Dialogue Detectives should observe and make notes on their own ideas, on things they agree and disagree with or on further questions they have. Alternatively, they can prepare to give feedback to the main group about the quality of the dialogue that took place and the group dynamics they observed.

Dialogue in the main group is carried on in the same way as it would be for the whole class, but students get more opportunity to speak as well as the opportunity to receive feedback from the Dialogue Detectives.

At some point during the dialogue (perhaps every ten to fifteen minutes), the Dialogue Detectives should change places with students from the main group so that they also get a turn to engage in the dialogue.

6.2 • CLUES TO DETECT: FOCUSING ON PERFORMANCE

> Dialogue Detectives need to be clear about the types of clues they are searching for.

Dialogue Detectives can focus on the performance of the participants in the dialogue and/or on the content of the dialogue itself. This section looks at the performance aspect of the dialogue.

When focusing on performance, the Dialogue Detectives should note examples of actions such as listening well to others, asking questions, supporting ideas with reasons, encouraging others, considering other points of view and responding. The following checklist should help them with this task:

In Appendix 1, you will also find this list in a format ready to be printed and distributed to your students.

1. Did people encourage each other to speak (e.g., encouraging gestures, taking turns)? (altruism)
2. Did people focus their attention on the speaker? (attentiveness)
3. Did people avoid interrupting or rushing the speaker? (patience)
4. Did people stick to their own convictions? (courage)
5. Did people keep their contributions brief? (concision)
6. Did people stick to the question? (tenacity and discipline)
7. Did people show a willingness to change their minds? (openness)
8. Did people listen carefully to ideas different from their own? (tolerance)
9. Did people recall others' ideas and put their names to them? (respect)
10. Did people try to build on others' ideas? (constructiveness)
11. Did people ask open and inviting questions? (curiosity)
12. Did people ask for clarification/definition of meaning? (precision)
13. Did people question assumptions or conclusions? (skepticism)
14. Did people ask for examples or evidence? (doubt)
15. Did people ask for reasons or criteria? (rationality)

16. Did people give examples or counter-examples? (realism)

17. Did people give reasons or justifications? (reasonableness)

18. Did people offer or explore alternative viewpoints? (creativity)

19. Did people make connections or analogies? (connectivity)

20. Did people make distinctions? (perceptiveness)

A simpler review sheet is shown in Figure 5. This might be more appropriate for younger students. Encourage your students to write YES in the appropriate box if they think they have achieved that particular goal or NO if they haven't. They should complete the right-hand column only after they have had a turn in the inner circle.

At the end, they can add up the number of YESs to arrive at a score. This is, of course, optional.

▶ **Figure 5: Dialogue Detectives Evidence Record**

	Dialogue Goals	Group	Myself
Productive	I spoke		
	Most people spoke		
	Helped others to speak		
	Concentrated for a whole session		
Collaborative	Listened carefully to every speaker		
	Let people finish saying what they wanted		
	Took turns to speak one at a time		
	Stuck with the main dialogue topics		
Meaningful	Tried to understand what others meant		
	Asked questions of myself and others		
	Identified similarities and differences		
Argumentative	Disagreed without showing anger		
	Tried to reach agreement where possible		
	Identified disagreements		
	Gave reasons		
	Score		

6.3 • CLUES TO DETECT: FOCUSING ON THINKING STRUCTURES

You can also get the students you've chosen to be Dialogue Detectives to focus on the thinking structures being used throughout the dialogue. For example:

1. Note anything anyone said that you agreed or disagreed with and give reasons.

2. Make a list of the opinions that arise and the reasons that support them.

3. Note any questions that occurred to you as you listened to the discussion.

4. Note any examples given in the discussion and say what they were examples of.

5. Note any counter-examples you can think of.

6. Note any alternative ideas not expressed in the discussion.

▶ Figure 6: **Thinking Structures**

Type of Thinking	Actions or Moves	Concepts
Productive	Generating ideas, generating alternative ideas, listing	Alternative, list, collection, class, category
Collaborative	Listening, taking turns, suspending judgment, establishing and applying ground rules	Community
Creating meaning	Questioning, classifying, comparing, ranking, connecting, clarifying, exemplifying, offering analogies, interpreting, summarizing, defining, elaborating	Same, different, principle, example, important, significant, special, ordinary, function, purpose, part, whole, multiple, single, complete, incomplete, class, category, all, some, none, many
Argumentative (Argument seen as the pursuit of truth rather than simply arguing as children might argue over a toy)	Agreeing, disagreeing, making an argument, questioning assumptions, assessing evidence	Opinion, belief, proposition, conclusion, claim, reason, premise, argument, cause, effect, symptom, consequence, true, false, agree, disagree, doubt, class, category, all, some, none, many, assumption, evidence, criteria, proof, judgment, justify
Speculative	Hypothesizing, predicting, imagining, offering thought experiments	Cause, effect, symptom, consequence, theory, hypothesis

6.4 • OTHER CLUES TO DETECT

You could also get the Dialogue Detectives to use the reasoning cards introduced in Figures 3 and 4 (in Chapter 4). For example, they could group the cards according to:

a. reasons used,

b. reasons not used,

c. reasons that could have been used but weren't.

Alternatively, they might hold up the relevant reasoning card when they think that a particular reasoning type is being used. For example, when they think an opinion is being expressed that is based on an assumption, they would hold up the Assumption/Opinion card. This might be done behind the scenes so that only you notice it. Alternatively, it could be done more publicly so as to draw the attention of their peers to it during the dialogue—or even to pause the dialogue for a period of reflection about the reasoning move. (Was it the appropriate move to make? Could the move have been made another way? Would there have been a more appropriate move to make?)

> Dialogue Detectives can also use the reasoning cards in Figures 3 and 4 (in Chapter 4) as a focus for the clues to gather.

6.5 • REVIEW

In this chapter we have explored the role of Dialogue Detectives. This is a very nice convention for doing the following:

1. Getting students to think more carefully about *how* a dialogue is running

2. Creating a period of metacognition (thinking about thinking) or metadialogue (thinking about the dialogue)

3. Giving students an opportunity to develop the habits of thinking about *how* they're thinking at the same time as considering *what* they are thinking during a dialogue

4. Knowing that there are Dialogue Detectives watching them—and particularly when they know what the clues are that the detectives are looking for—very often makes those taking part in the dialogue more attentive, deliberate and more likely to use dialogue moves

6.6 • NEXT STEPS AND FURTHER READING

Here are some suggestions for what you could do next so that you get the most out of this chapter:

1. Try out a Dialogue Detectives session with your students, and then reflect on the relative success of the approach (reflect with your students for the greatest impact).

2. Agree on a different set of clues for each Dialogue Detective, and then get them to share their findings with each other.

3. Read Chapter 8 on Learning Detectives in *Challenging Learning Through Feedback* (Nottingham & Nottingham, 2017), which forms part of the Challenging Learning series.

> "The whole purpose of democracy is that we may hold counsel with one another, so as not to depend upon the understanding of one man, but to depend upon the counsel of all."
>
> (Wilson, 2014)

DIALOGUE STRUCTURES

7.0 • PREVIEW

This chapter includes an outline of some useful cooperative learning structures that encourage dialogue, including these:

- Corners

- Pairs

- Think-Pair-Share (and Think-Write-Share-Compare)

- Opinion Lines and Concept Lines

- Talking Heads and Jigsaw Groups

All of the strategies are excellent ways to engage your students in collaborative dialogue. They are also easy to put into practice and will give your students the chance to be a bit more active than in many traditional forms of dialogue.

> Dialogue structures are useful tools for engaging and focusing students' attention.

7.1 • PAIRED DIALOGUE

In Pairs

Directing students to talk in pairs is so common that it hardly seems worth mentioning. It differs from Think-Pair-Share in that pairs aren't always given any initial thinking time and may not be asked to share with other students at the end. You simply ask pairs to share their thoughts with a partner on a task,

> Structures for paired dialogue include Think-Pair-Share and Think-Write-Share-Compare.

question or problem. The main use of this strategy is to get students thinking. It is often said that people don't know their thoughts until they have expressed them. This structure compels students to prompt each other to express their thoughts and, in so doing, discover what they really think.

After each pair has worked on a question or task, you can team them up with another pair to summarize what they discussed. Prompt them to discuss similarities and differences between each pair's summary. Afterward the fours can divide back into two pairs and perhaps team up with another pair.

Think-Pair-Share

Ask your students a question or give them a task. Then give them individual thinking time. After that, ask your students to get together with a partner to discuss and develop their ideas. After a reasonable amount of time, give each pair a chance to share their thinking with the whole group. Take as many responses from pairs as time allows.

Think-Write-Share-Compare

A variation of Think-Pair-Share is Think-Write-Share-Compare. For this structure, ask your students a question or set them a task and get each one to write down their initial ideas independently of each other. Then pair your students up and ask them to read out their ideas to each other. The discussion in pairs should then focus on the similarities and differences between their ideas.

If you collect your students' writing at the end, it can give you useful insight into their thinking and provide you with ideas for future lessons.

7.2 • OPINION LINES

Opinion Lines are very useful for beginning to explore statements using examples, gauging degrees of agreement and disagreement or identifying degrees of preference.

Opinion Lines are useful for exploring the relative degree of agreement and disagreement.

As with the Opinion Corners activity (see Section 7.3), you should begin by inviting your students to take an initial stance and to discuss their choice with the people around them, making sure to give their reasons. The difference with Opinion Lines is that they allow for more nuanced responses than do Corners because there is the opportunity to compare *degrees* of agreement or disagreement.

Opinion Lines give your students the opportunity to:

- show (literally) where they stand on an issue,
- see the spread of opinion in the group,
- think critically about their own and others' views,
- demonstrate changes in opinion through physical movement.

Setting Up an Opinion Line

1. Create a line long enough for all your students to stand along. It might help to mark this with a rope or some string.

2. Mark one end with a Completely Agree sign and the other with a Completely Disagree sign. Talk through the other descriptors shown in Figure 7 if you think it will help your students understand the degrees of agreement and disagreement.

▶ **Figure 7: Opinion Line Diagram**

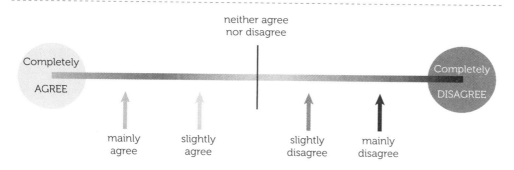

3. Formulate a statement that expresses a point of view relating to the topic your students are in dialogue about. Make it bold and contentious to increase the likelihood of everyone having an opinion. For example:

   - We should celebrate Christmas four times per year.
   - School should start with two hours of sports every day.
   - All bullies should be banned from school.
   - Bullies should have their mobile devices taken away for three weeks.
   - Mobile devices should be given free to all students.
   - Mobile devices should be banned in all schools.
   - Students should be paid to go to school.
   - Everyone should be made to eat at least eight portions of fruit or vegetables per day.
   - All violent dogs should be put down.
   - Sixteen-year-olds should be allowed to drive cars.
   - Teenagers should not be allowed to get a lift in a car driven by another teenager (since this is one of the most likely causes of death in sixteen- to twenty-four-year olds in developed countries).
   - Hamlet was a flawed character.

4. Explain to your students that you are going to give them a contentious statement to think about. Say they will have time to think about it first; then you will ask them to stand on the part of the line that corresponds with how much they agree or disagree with the statement.

5. Once your students have taken a place on the line, get them to talk with the people around them to compare their reasons for standing where they are. The

> Here are some useful topics for introducing Opinion Lines to students.

following prompts should help them ensure their conversation is more exploratory (see Section 2.6.3) than cumulative (see Section 2.6.1):

- What do you think?
- What are your reasons?
- I agree with you because . . .
- I disagree with you because . . .
- Is there another way of looking at this?
- What if . . . ?
- Have we considered all the factors?
- What have we agreed on?

6. An extension of this is to get students to pair up with someone from a very different part of the line. You could get your students to choose their partner, or you could orchestrate it in the way shown in Figure 8.

▶ Figure 8: **Comparing Different Opinions Along an Opinion Line**

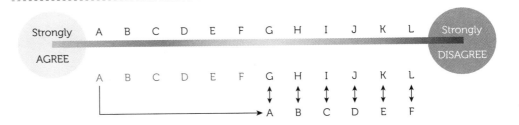

Notice that in this opinion line, we have chosen the labels Strongly Agree and Strongly Disagree as these might sometimes be more appropriate than Completely Agree and Completely Disagree as used in Figure 7.

7. Thinking language that might help with opinion lines include the following:

fact	reason	evidence	opinion	assumption
persuade	reliable	agree	convince	disagree
exception	if/then	example	conclusion	argument

8. The following are a few alternative ways to set up an opinion line:

Alternative 1: Read out an item and ask just a few of your students to decide how they would respond. Once the chosen few have decided where to stand on the line, you can then invite other students to ask them questions about their positions. The questions might explore reasons and alternative ideas. Ask the students on the line to move if at any point their opinion changes in response to the comments and questions from their classmates.

Alternative 2: Combine opinion lines with role-play. Your students could take the roles of characters and position themselves according to how they think the characters would respond. They could answer questions in character.

Alternative 3: Give different groups different opinion lines. For example, split your students into three groups and give each group one of the three opinion lines in Figure 9.

▶ Figure 9: Variations of Opinion Lines

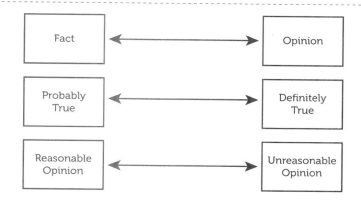

Now give the *same* statement to all three groups, irrespective of which opinion line they are being asked to stand on.

For example, you could use the statement "Stealing is wrong." One group can then consider if this is a fact or an opinion; the second group should consider if it is probably true or definitely true; the third group can think about whether it is a reasonable opinion or an unreasonable opinion. This in itself can create an interesting dialogue about the differences in responses between groups.

Here are some more example statements for you to use:

- It is against the law to steal.
- Robin Hood was right to steal from the rich to give to the poor.
- Robin Hood was a moral man.
- It is good to share.
- If a teacher confiscates something from you, then this is not stealing.
- More people will go to the moon in the twenty-first century than went in the twentieth century.
- Religion has been the root cause for many wars.
- Sunshine is good for you.
- Too much sunshine is bad for you.
- Serial killers should receive the death sentence.

7.3 • OPINION CORNERS

Opinion Corners have a similar structure to Opinion Lines and so can be introduced in a similar way. The main difference is that using the Corners will prevent your students from "sitting on the fence" because Corners requires them to choose from one of four descriptors: strongly agree, agree, disagree, strongly disagree. Set up Opinion Corners as shown in Figure 10.

> Opinion Corners require an exact choice, whereas Opinion Lines allow students to "sit on the fence."

► Figure 10: Opinion Corners

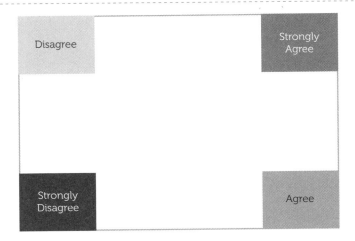

After you read a statement (examples are given below), your students should stand in the corner that best represents their opinion on the matter. Tell them they have to choose one of the corners. They cannot stand somewhere in the middle. They must make a decision as to the one that is the best description of their opinion. They are allowed to move if they change their minds, but even then they should move from one corner to another rather than to the middle or off to a side somewhere.

Once your students have chosen a corner, get them to talk about their choice with the people around them. After that, get a spokesperson from each corner to give a summary of the reasons why the people in their corner made the choice they did. This will give your students a chance to hear different perspectives on the issue.

Statements for Opinion Corners

Here are some statements to get you started with Opinion Corners.

Here are some useful starter topics for introducing Opinion Corners to students.

- It is wrong to steal.
- You must never talk to strangers.
- Students should never have to take tests.
- Parents should be fined if they take their children on holiday during school term time.
- Students should be allowed to listen to their own music during lessons.
- Violent video games are a bad influence on young people and should be banned.
- The big, bad wolf wasn't really bad. He was just misunderstood.
- Footballers are paid too much money.
- Poverty is the parent of revolution and crime. (Aristotle)
- We cannot all succeed when half of us are held back. (Malala Yousafzai)
- Everyone in the world should be made to speak Spanish as well as their own language.
- Education is the most powerful weapon you can use to change the world. (Nelson Mandela)

The Benefits of Opinion Corners

(Martin) In comparison to Opinion Lines, Opinion Corners emphasize the different views everyone holds and introduce quite distinct groupings. For that reason, Opinion Corners are very useful in developing not only skills of reasoning and explanation but also the language of persuasion.

The benefit of tasks such as these is that students are actively involved in building their own understanding. When using these strategies with students, we have often noticed how the opinions and reasons of others stay with the students for longer. Because they actively process the information (physically and cognitively), the students retain it for longer. This is a real benefit in developing the use of Opinion Corners in the classroom and I often use it as a precursor of written argument.

Ask your students to structure an assignment around the responses given during an Opinion Corners activity. For example, set up the Opinion Corners with a statement such as "The British were against the slave trade." The students go to the corner that best represents their opinion, give reasons for their choices and listen to the views of others.

The students can then structure their written assignment according to what they have heard in the activity.

> Paragraph 1: I agree that (the British were against the slave trade) because (give a key reason from their corner).
>
> Paragraph 2: In addition, people might also suggest that (give further reasons from their corner).
>
> Paragraph 3: However, other people disagree. They say (give reasons from the disagree corner).
>
> Paragraph 4: Whereas other people would argue that (give reasons from one or both of the remaining corners).
>
> Paragraph 5: So in conclusion, while some people would say (make statement), I believe that (make personal statement) because (give reasons).

This structure for written work can be reinforced—especially with older students—during the Opinion Corners activity by having flipchart paper or sticky notes in each corner for the students to write their opinions on. The whole class can then move around and read the selection of opinions, rather than just sharing verbally.

> **These open, challenging tasks engage interest and encourage respect for others' points of view, building a climate in which the students more readily recognize and value the opinions of others and see collaborative talk and diversity as valuable opportunities for learning. Take advantage of this diversity by encouraging the students to reflect on all the reasons they have heard and to move corners if they wish. This emphasizes to the students that it is okay to hear different opinions and change your mind, which is also a good indicator that students are making progress in thinking and understanding.**

If a student moves corners, it is a great opportunity to ask the student what they heard that made them change their mind. This encourages the idea of persuasive language, can add to students' verbal and written vocabulary and reinforces the idea that reflection is part of successful learning. Written vocabulary can then be built on further by asking questions such as "How would you encourage other people to come to your corner?"

Opinion Corners lend themselves better than Opinion Lines to the development of persuasive language.

An additional bonus with Opinion Corners is that it places the teacher in the direct role of mediator—supporting, prompting and questioning the process of learning, rather than giving answers. As the only person who is allowed to stand in the middle of the room, the teacher is, quite literally, the only person with "no opinion." Placing ourselves in this position emphasizes the role of the teacher as facilitator, rather than the font of all knowledge.

7.4 • CHOOSING CORNERS

> Options for Opinion Corners always range from strongly agree to strongly disagree, whereas Choosing Corners offers the flexibility to assign different items to each corner (e.g., questions, images or concepts).

This structure uses Corners again, but this time the focus isn't on opinion; rather, it is on giving reasons for a choice. The items might be questions, statements, concepts, situations, images, arguments and so on.

For example:

- Choose the question you most want to discuss.
- Choose the statement you agree with (or disagree with) most.
- Choose the concept you want to explore or create questions about.
- Choose the situation you would rather be in.
- Choose the item you think is most important.
- Choose the image you like most.

Example for Younger Students

> Here are some useful starter topics for introducing Choosing Corners to young students.

Put photographs of a drink (e.g., water), a fast food (e.g., pizza), the sun and a fruit (e.g., an apple) in each of four corners (one photo per corner). Then ask the following questions:

1. Which is the healthiest one?
2. Which one would your parents say you should not have too much of?
3. Which one would you like to have lots of at a party?
4. Which one would be nicest to have on a school day?
5. Which one would be nicest to have on a holiday?

Example for Older Students

> Here are some useful starter topics for introducing Choosing Corners to older students.

Put photographs of different-sized settlements (e.g., hamlet, village, town, city) or different artworks in each of four corners (one photo per corner). Then ask questions such as the following:

For the settlements

1. Where are you most likely to find happy people?
2. Which one is the best to live in if you're a child? A parent? An old person?
3. Where would you hear the most noise during the day? During the night?

For the artwork

1. Which one is the saddest? Which is the most joyful?
2. Which one do you think took longest to paint?

3. Which one makes the strongest statement about . . . (e.g., feminism, war, politics)?

Give your students thinking time to make their choice. Encourage them to move around the room, considering each option. Then ask them to go to their chosen corners and share with others who have chosen the same corner why they have made that particular choice. If a large number of students are in the same corner, then they could split into pairs or threes. After a short while, invite a spokesperson from each group to explain the group's thinking. As each group does this, draw attention to the similarities and differences of the reasons given. In particular, highlight any contradictions or inconsistencies.

The benefit of this activity is that it gets students moving around the room and therefore changes the dynamic (and maybe even the thinking). It also gives you the opportunity to draw attention more clearly to the differing opinions among your students.

7.5 • TALKING HEADS

One of the problems with small-group dialogues is that some students may opt out if they feel they are not being listened to or if another participant is dominating. *Talking Heads* is a good way to reduce the chance of this happening.

> Talking Heads increases students' attention by giving the impression that anyone can be picked at any time to speak.

To begin with, split your students into groups of three or four and ask them to identify themselves with numbers (one, two, three, four). Check to see that they know what their number is. If there are some groups with one less than the norm, then give one person two numbers. If there are some groups with one more than the norm, then give two people the same number.

Once students are in their groups, give them a question or task to tackle.

After a period of discussion, stop all the groups and focus their attention on you. Now call out a number and ask all those students identified with that number to report back on what their group discussed.

If they discussed more than one item, the process can be repeated with further numbers so that different students complete the report back.

The students' perceptions of the randomness of the number calling encourages them all to take responsibility for being prepared and helping each other become prepared to answer. It is also a time-effective way of having a plenary session because not all students give feedback but all have contributed in their groups.

7.6 • JIGSAW GROUPS

Jigsaw Grouping is another good way to stop some students opting out of dialogue activities. Assigning each student a "jigsaw" piece of information will ensure all your students are dependent upon each other in order for everyone to succeed.

> Jigsaw Groups give each student the responsibility of being the "expert" for their part of the jigsaw.

Jigsaw Groups were designed by social psychologist Elliot Aronson to help weaken racial cliques in forcibly integrated schools.

Here is a slightly adapted explanation for Jigsaw Groups from the website Jigsaw Classroom (www.jigsaw.org).

Jigsaw in Eight Easy Steps

1. Divide your students into groups of five. These are the home groups.

2. Divide the activity into five segments. For example, if you want history students to learn about Anne Frank, you might divide a short biography of her into stand-alone segments on (1) her early life; (2) the period before going into hiding; (3) life in her hiding place; (4) arrest, deportation and death; (5) her legacy.

3. Give each home group one of the segments to read. Give them time to question each other, discuss difficult words and make notes.

4. Ask each student in the home group to number themselves one to five.

5. Person 1 from each home group then moves to sit with all the other number 1s. Person 2 sits with all other number 2s on another table and so on. These new groups are the away groups.

6. Each member of the away group takes it in turn to present his or her segment to the other students in this new group. By sharing the information that they are expert in, the whole group develops a picture of the full topic.

7. Once all of the information has been shared in the away group, the students can return to their home group and share what they have learned about the other segments.

8. Each of the students now knows about one aspect of the topic in depth and the whole topic in breadth. A quiz can be given to help the students realize how much they have learned about the whole topic from their dialogue with each other.

7.7 • CLUSTERING

> Clustering is a good way to get students moving and making links.

Clustering is an effective activity for promoting active and engaged dialogue around a theme or concept. It is also a good way to get your students into different groupings from normal.

1. Give each of your students a card with a different statement or fact relating to the key concept or theme. For example, if your theme is "weather," then you could use the following cards:

Sun	Infiltration
Rain	Hail
Snow	Ice
Evaporation	Lake
Precipitation	Sea
Condensation	Vegetation
Transpiration	Soil
Runoff	Wind

Or if you are just looking to group your students relatively randomly, then you could give each of them one of these sports cards:

Football	Badminton
Baseball	Track
Handball	Hurdles

Soccer	Cycling
Tennis	Rowing
Swimming	Sailing
Hockey	Climbing
Karate	Parachuting

2. Once all your students have read their card and are confident they understand it, ask them to move around the room and find links with other cards. Once they have found links with other cards, then they should cluster together to form groups. If a group gets too big, then it might need to break up into subgroups.

3. Your students should be able to clearly identify what connects each of the cards in their group. For example, if the students holding the cards with rain, snow, hail and ice have clustered together, then they should be able to say their connection is types of precipitation. Or if a group has come together with cards saying swimming, karate, track and hurdles, then they might say these are all sports that do not require a bat or a ball. Of course, these are just examples. The students could have grouped themselves in different ways and indeed could have given different reasons for the same groupings (e.g., rain, snow, hail and ice are all states of water or they are all expected in winter).

4. Once all of your students have clustered into groups, challenge them on their reasoning, assumptions and choices. For example, "Why have you not included card x in your group as that also fits your criterion?"

5. Each cluster can now be the dialogue groupings going forward into the next activity you have planned for your students.

7.8 • REVIEW

In this chapter we have explored various structures for dialogue. They are easy to put into practice and will offer your students opportunities to talk in structured ways that involve moving around or talking with different partners.

The sorts of questions you can encourage your students to ask during their paired and small-group dialogues include the following:

- What do you think?

- What are your reasons?

- I agree with you because . . .

- I disagree with you because . . .

- Is there another way of looking at this?

- What if . . . ?

- Have we considered all the factors?

- What have we agreed?

The language that will help them express themselves more accurately includes *fact, reason, evidence, opinion, assumption, persuade, reliable, agree, disagree, convince, exception, if / then, example, conclusion* and *argument*.

7.9 • NEXT STEPS AND FURTHER READING

Here are some suggestions for what you could do next so that you get the most out of this chapter:

1. Try out all the strategies in a series of lessons over a two-week period.

2. Record your reflections to each of these in the Repertoire and Judgment Notes section at the back of the book. Which worked best? Did different students react more positively to some strategies than to others?

3. Ask your colleagues if they have any variations on these dialogue structures, such as the Think-Write-Share-Compare version of Think-Pair-Share.

Some of the dialogue structures we have shared have been popularized by the cooperative learning movement, in particular, Robert Slavin and Spencer Kagan.

1. A good short summary of the work of Robert Slavin can be found in an article on using cooperative learning structures by Dr. Tzu-Pu Wang (2009): http://bit .ly/190RNnB.

2. There are many free resources on the Internet about the use of Kagan's structures. A good summary in book form is *Cooperative Learning Structures* by Kagan (2013).

> "We only think when confronted with a problem."
>
> (Dewey, 1916/2011)

MYSTERIES

8.0 • PREVIEW

(James) Mysteries started as a popular teaching strategy among humanities teachers (geography, history, religious education, English) in schools in North East England. I am delighted to say I was one of the original members in the 1990s of the Northumberland Thinking Skills in the Humanities Project during which many of these strategies were developed. The other authors of this book—Martin Renton and Jill Nottingham—also went on to work full-time as teaching and learning consultants making extensive use of Mysteries and all the other strategies mentioned in this book. More recently, Martin has also developed these strategies for use with college students, and Jill has adapted them for use with early years children.

David Leat and Adam Nichols, two professors from Newcastle University, coined the term *mystery* when working with the Northumberland teachers to refer to an activity where students use a set of clues to find a reasoned answer to a central question. The information in these clues can be text, images, objects, charts or a mix of all of these. Mysteries can be used in all areas of the curriculum.

In this chapter we explain how to use a Mystery to develop dialogue with your students. We also provide three examples to get you started.

> Mysteries engage students in dialogue about a topic relevant to their lives.

8.1 • MYSTERIES

> **A Mystery is a problem-solving activity based on a central question that is open to more than one reasonable answer.**

The information or clues needed to answer the question should be presented on separate slips of paper so that your students can analyze, sort, sequence and link them together.

The questions at the heart of Mysteries are most often matters of interpretation, judgment and argument. They tend to involve dialogues on causation or speculation about consequences.

Here are some key principles to follow when creating a Mystery:

1. Choose a character or primary focus to center your Mystery on.
2. Choose a key question or dilemma.
3. Create some ambiguous information to support different possible answers to the question.
4. Ensure some of the information is irrelevant and some is contradictory.
5. Make sure there are some "red herrings" to detract from an obvious answer.
6. Make sure there are links or connections between some parts of the information provided.
7. Make the character and subject relevant to the group you are working with.

> The key principle of a Mystery is the focus on a central character that students can identify with.

8.2 • RUNNING A MYSTERY

> The Challenging Learning team are writing new Mysteries all the time. Three examples can be found in this book, with many more online.

A. Setup

Choose a Mystery to use with your students; there are three in this chapter or you could write your own (see Section 8.6).

Print a set of clues for each group. Split your students into groups of approximately four. Each group will need their own set of clues.

Depending on the particular Mystery, the clues will come in either first, second and third batches or just in one big batch. This will be made clear at the beginning of each of the Mysteries included in this book and those available online.

> Students need time to explore the pieces of evidence within a Mystery.

B. Exploration Phase

Ask each group to lay all the clues you have given out on the table in front of them. Once they have read through each one, get them to group, connect or in some way sort the clues. This movement is a crucial feature of the task, contributing in large measure to its effectiveness as a classroom strategy for thinking.

Remind all your students:

1. This is a group activity, so everyone in the group should be taking an active role.

2. They should choose categories for their clues. This might include relevant/irrelevant, personal/background, fact/opinion, supporting/contradictory and so on. Do *not* impose these categories—they should come up with their own categories, as this is an important part of the learning process.

3. Mysteries are all about dialogue. So there should be lots of talk, including explanation, reasoning, counter-examples, challenges and questioning.

4. When moving slips of paper around, your students should always give each other an explanation for why. They should not let anyone take over and do all the sorting and classifying without seeking the opinions and responses of others.

5. The task is an open one and may have quite a few possible right answers. If they are doing it correctly, then they may often change their minds when they see fresh connections or spot logical patterns they hadn't noticed before.

> For all Mysteries, the process is more important than the answer.

C. Comparison of Strategy

After your students have had enough time in their groups to process and begin categorizing the clues, ask each group to explain their strategy to the whole class. This should highlight some differences in approach and therefore provide cause for reflection.

D. Main Activity

After your students have had chance to hear what strategies and categories other groups are using, they should begin to move more definitely toward answering the key question. (For example, see Section 8.9.3, Mystery: Is Sally a Good Friend?). As they do this, remind them to make good use of these thinking and dialogue skills:

> There are many ways for groups to sift through the information presented within a Mystery. Students should be encouraged to compare these differences with each other.

- sorting relevant information
- interpreting information
- using inference and deduction skills
- making links between the clues
- speculating to form hypotheses

- checking and refining
- explaining, reasoning and justifying
- problem solving
- decision making

As you circulate around the groups, use some of the following terms:

inquire	infer	plan	link/connect	refine
probable	analyze	hypothesize	conclude	data
evidence	possible	sequence	predict	certain

> Remind students to use thinking terms such as *predict, possible* and *infer* when engaging in a Mystery.

For example, you might say some of these things to particular groups:

- Which pieces of information have you linked or connected?
- Which of those pieces are more probable than others?
- What is your hypothesis in terms of the sequence of events?
- What do you infer from this piece of data?

You will know when the main activity phase is drawing to a close when each group begins to draw some conclusions. The best situation will be that your students offer their conclusions with an air of open-mindedness, in the knowledge that their conclusions aren't quite definite. If, on the other hand, they seem very sure about their ideas, then you should try to create at least some uncertainty through questioning and drawing their attention to conflicting pieces of evidence.

E. Presentations and Reflection

Ask each group to present their findings to the whole class. To ensure that all students get a fair chance to speak (rather than just the more dominant characters), you might want to use the Talking Heads method of selection as described in Section 7.5.

As each group presents their conclusions, encourage all the other groups to identify similarities and differences when compared with their own findings.

The differences might be to do with *content* (for example, "We agreed that Bjørn should seize the day and move to France; otherwise it would be a waste of his talent. The other group thought he should stay out of obligation to his sick father"). Or they might be to do with *process* (for example, "We divided our clues into relevant, irrelevant and could be relevant, whereas the group presenting their findings split their clues into personal, background and red herrings").

After each group has presented their conclusions, use some of the following metacognitive questions to review the learning journey:

1. What information helped you?

2. Which clues were misleading?

3. How did you categorize the clues? If you were to do this again, what categories would you go for next time?

4. What role did you play within your group? In what way would you act or think differently next time?

5. What degree of certainty do you have about your group's conclusion?

6. Is uncertainty a good thing? How does it make you feel? What are its benefits?

> When groups present their findings, they should be reminded to talk about how they made their decisions as well as what they decided.

8.3 • MYSTERIES IN PRACTICE

> Here is an example of how a Mystery might work in practice.

Here is a set of reflections from an article by David Leat (2002) about the common responses to Mysteries.

Exploration

Pupils in small groups have been presented with an unsorted mixture of useful and misleading data. The groups familiarize themselves with data items. Some groups will decide to distribute the slips to be read aloud in turn before laying them out. Others just spread them out, neatly or otherwise. In this stage group members read the text and register the presence of a slip that someone else has read aloud. Some groups will need help from the teacher to infer any meaning from the slips.

Pupils share some first thoughts about the meanings and relative significance of the items. They often begin to organize the data into sets on the basis of perceived common characteristics, suggesting a general strategy based on association. Low achieving groups frequently form sets on the basis of common vocabulary such as the names of characters, animals or places. Most groups assemble broad thematic sets—for example "anything to do with earthquakes" or data items suggesting a chain of events. On the tables, these sets are usually arranged as columns and blocks. This stage indicates a developing familiarity with subject matter. A refinement is the creation of subsets, which may be triggered by one thematic set growing so large that the group begins to reclassify the items. It is generally the more able groups who form sets based on the background data, although at this stage they may not appreciate its full significance.

All groups form a reject pile. There appears to be a further contrast between higher and lower achieving groups in that higher achieving groups are more inclined to reconsider their reject pile, while some lower achieving groups never look at them again. There is a role for the teacher here in prompting these groups to consider (and reconsider) all options.

The Main Activity

Some groups need help to get beyond the setting stage, even though the sets they have formed may be quite limited in terms of producing an answer. However, the majority of groups begin to identify relationships between sets or between single data items. In some instances this is in lines representing the construction of a causal explanation (sequencing), while in others it is a nonlinear pattern representing multiple inter-relationships (webbing). Inference is common in the production of these patterns.

This stage can be radical or modest and can take many forms. It may start with the movement of a single slip from one set to another but can include the reintroduction of reject slips or wholesale movement and regrouping of items and sets. These reworkings appear to represent the establishment of new sets of relationships, which are increasingly abstract and likely to include the background data items. In the reworking process, moved data items are cumulatively taking on new meanings. It is our impression that the more the data is rearranged, the better the quality of any subsequent written work. High ability groups show little reluctance in breaking their original sequences and webs, while other groups may be very frustrated by having to do so. Many groups do not rework.

For a few groups, the physical manipulation ceases but the discussion continues. It is possible that they have internalized the data to a point where they can explore new relationships and hypotheses without recourse to the concrete format of the data slips.

8.4 • QUESTIONING CAUSE AND EFFECT WITHIN MYSTERIES

One way to help deepen the inquiry as your students engage in a Mystery is to focus on cause and effect. A cause is part or all of an explanation of why something (an effect) has happened. For example:

Question: Why did John fall on his way to school? (*effect*)

Answer: Because he stepped on a banana skin. (*cause*)

Mysteries provide an excellent context for students to learn the difference between cause and effect.

First, we should say that there could be *more than one* cause of John falling on the way to school. We know he slipped on a banana skin, but it might also be that John is clumsy and therefore this increases the likelihood that John slipped on anything that happened to be in his way.

Second, the banana skin had to be there before John could slip on it. So maybe the fall was caused less by the banana skin itself and more by the people involved in the banana skin being there in the first place. For example, the cause might have something to do with the banana growers, the exporters, the seller or the consumer.

This second set of reasons has more to do with conditions than causes. Conditions are those things that an effect couldn't have happened without. "Bananas are sold in shops" is a condition. John wouldn't have slipped on one if they weren't there to be sold.

So can we say that banana selling is a cause of John falling on the way to school? Possible answers might include the following:

- No, because a cause must have a stronger connection. Many bananas are sold that don't cause accidents, so the connection between banana selling and slipping isn't strong.

- Causes are things that fit in with patterns. People who buy bananas don't normally fall over. People who step on them often do. There is a pattern.

- In science, things are most often chosen as causes if scientists can repeat the causes and effects, all other things being equal. If the same weight was put on a banana skin and given the same kind of push, would it always slip?

- Not everything can be repeated in an experiment. But we can guess that causes are things that could be changed or could have been different. They might be out of the ordinary. So John walked to school every day, but he didn't fall over. Then one day he did something different—he stepped on a banana skin. The different thing is likely to be the cause.

- Causes are often the last things that happen before the effect. Ask what John did just before he fell.

- First look at the conditions and then use your judgment to choose the ones that seem most likely to have caused the effect.

- Some causes can seem more important if they are things that people do deliberately. If John slipped on a banana skin, we could say the skin caused him to fall. If Peter threw it in John's way deliberately, we would say the most important cause was that Peter threw it.

8.5 • REVIEWING A MYSTERY USING THE SOLO TAXONOMY

The Structure of Observed Learning Outcomes (SOLO) taxonomy is a model that describes levels of increasing complexity in students' understanding of subjects. It was proposed by John B. Biggs and K. Collis and has since gained popularity. We have written about it in depth in *Challenging Learning Through Feedback* (Nottingham & Nottingham, 2017).

As a reflection tool, it can really help you decide how much depth of understanding your students have been able to reach during a Mystery (see Figure 11).

SOLO Level	Performance Level
Prestructural	Students select some clues that may be relevant but cannot develop an explanation.
Unistructural	Students select one or two clues that are relevant and develop an explanation but do not fully address the question.
Multistructural	Students select several clues and develop an explanation, but it does not fully address the question. There may be some limited links made between some of the clues, but they are not all linked together to reach a successful conclusion.
Relational	Students select several clues that are likely to be grouped in some way. The explanation has clear causal connections such as *because, and then* and *meanwhile*. The question is answered successfully.
Extended abstract	In addition to the above, students use wider knowledge to help interpret the information and make more general and abstract statements. They are able to entertain more than one solution and are more likely to identify flaws or weaknesses in their own reasoning.

> The SOLO taxonomy is well known for drawing attention to the significance of surface-level and deep-level understanding. As such, it is a very useful tool for reviewing how well students have engaged in a Mystery.

8.6 • WRITING YOUR OWN MYSTERIES

1. Identify a theme relevant to your students that will lend itself to inquiry. Make sure there is something in the theme that can be problematized and personalized in a narrative. For example, if your students are studying a topic about transport, then you could create a Mystery about "Why did Mr. and Mrs. Brown sell their car?"

2. Make a set of fifteen to thirty slips that provide the necessary information. Continuing with the Browns' car example, a set of slips might include the following:

   Seven or eight background or context clues (e.g., a photo of Mrs. Brown's driving license; an insurance quote; a statistic about driving in their home town; wage information for the couple; information about the VW emissions scandal; information about the method for measuring carbon emissions; something about worldwide agreements to reduce the amount of carbon emissions)

   Five or six possible causes of change (e.g., the negative results from an eye exam; information about a proposal to increase car tax; one of the Browns' children joining an environmental group; a headline that the price of oil has hit a record high; information about a new metro station opening within walking distance of the Browns' home; tickets for an expensive round-the-world cruise)

   Five or six possible reactions or effects of change (e.g., an application to join the local leisure center; a copy of an email sent by Mrs. Brown saying how proud she is that her son has joined Greenpeace; an advert for the sale of their car)

   Three to five red herrings to confuse (e.g., nuclear energy facts; a story about Russia pulling out of the latest worldwide environmental talks; the formula for combustion; the performance statistics for a different car from the one the Browns' currently own)

   One to three pieces of irrelevant information (e.g., Mr. Brown's favorite food; Mrs. Brown's favorite hobby is knitting; the name of their cat)

3. Remember to vary the level of complexity and the form of the information so that all your students can play a role in solving the Mystery.

8.7 • REVIEW

In this chapter, we have explored the idea of Mysteries. The main points have included:

1. Mysteries are open-ended and may have quite a few possible "right" answers. Students are encouraged to use as much of the data as possible in formulating their explanation.

2. Mysteries have a strong narrative thread—they are about people involved in significant events. This personalization of the event helps to pique the interest of all students.

3. Some of the information relates to place and time; some information is very concrete and visible, whereas other information is more abstract and relates to possible background factors.

4. Not all of the information is necessarily relevant. Some items are included as red herrings, making the task inherently and deliberately open and ambiguous.

8.8 • NEXT STEPS AND FURTHER READING

Here are some suggestions for what you could do next so that you get the most out of this chapter:

1. Try out one of the Mysteries described in the next few pages with at least two different groups.

2. Compare the outcomes of each trial, and identify what worked and what needs improving.

3. Have a go at writing a new Mystery. Ensure that there are clues that fit the following categories: relevant and irrelevant, supporting and contradictory, plus one or two diversionary clues (red herrings).

Mysteries are introduced and used extensively in the following books:

- Baumfield, V., & Leat, D. (Eds.). (2002). *Thinking through religious education.* Cambridge, UK: Chris Kington.

- Fisher, P., Wilkinson, I., & Leat, D. (Eds.). (2000). *Thinking through history.* Cambridge, UK: Chris Kington.

- Harbottle, C., Barlow, G., & Leat, D. (Eds.). (2007). *Thinking through PSHE.* Cambridge, UK: Chris Kington.

- Higgins, S., Baumfield, V., & Leat, D. (Eds.). (2000). *Thinking through primary teaching.* Cambridge, UK: Chris Kington.

- Leat, D. (2001). *Thinking through geography* (2nd ed.). Cambridge, UK: Chris Kington.

- Wright, D., Taverner, S., & Leat, D. (Eds.). (2009). *Thinking through mathematics.* Cambridge, UK: Chris Kington.

8.9.1 • MYSTERY: SHOULD BJØRN MOVE TO FRANCE?

By Mark Bollom

I designed this Mystery to explore the concepts of life choices and opportunity with my thirteen- to sixteen-year-old students. The Mystery encourages students to examine themes such as these:

- risk and reward
- chance and fortune
- ethics and morals
- social and economic security
- life choices

The main character, Bjørn Larsen, is faced with a choice between accepting an offer to ride professionally for French cycle team FDJ or to stay in Norway with his family. If he chooses the latter, then he could receive coaching and financial support through the state-funded Elite Development Programme. There are, of course, many other considerations for Bjørn and the students to take into account before reaching a conclusion.

Background information about the Tour de France can be found at www.letour.com, including all the past winners (www.letour.fr/HISTO/us/TDF/recherche/FRA/all/victoires .html).

Using the Bjørn Mystery With Your Students

Age range: 13+

Key Words

Opportunity, decision making, duty, responsibility, sacrifice, choice, dreams, aspirations, goals, risk, reward, security, selfish, single-minded, driven, familiarity, unfamiliarity, life-changing, safe, cost, unintended consequences, ideas, ambitions, morals, ethics

Learning Intention

To consider an individual's life choices and decisions when striving to fulfill personal ambition

Success Criteria

To reach the learning goal, students will:

- think about the concept of life choices
- be able to describe the personal and social implications of life choices
- question each other's suggestions when in dialogue with each other about life choices

Before giving out the first set of cards to your students, tell them a little about Bjørn (see the intro above). Do *not* explain too much! Your introduction should whet their appetite and generate some questions that your students would like to find answers to; it should not tell them everything they need to know (otherwise the cards will become obsolete!). Once they've had time to sort the cards (using their own criteria), then you can give them Set B.

▶ Figure 12: Bjørn Mystery (Set A)

QUESTION: Should Bjørn move to France?	QUESTION: Should Bjørn move to France?
Bjørn's ambition is to wear the yellow jersey in cycling's most prestigious event – the Tour de France. ©2015 www.challenginglearning.com	Bjørn's grandmother was French. ©2015 www.challenginglearning.com
QUESTION: Should Bjørn move to France?	QUESTION: Should Bjørn move to France?
Bjørn has been Norway's Under 18 national road race champion. ©2015 www.challenginglearning.com	Bjørn's father had the opportunity to ride professionally when he was in his early 20s but decided instead to focus on his career in medicine. ©2015 www.challenginglearning.com
QUESTION: Should Bjørn move to France?	QUESTION: Should Bjørn move to France?
When he was young Bjørn visited France with his mother and father. They stayed in a hotel because his father was at a seminar. Bjørn remembers hating the food and thought all the adults he met were unfriendly. ©2015 www.challenginglearning.com	Bjørn went to the Norwegian College of Elite Sport (Norges Toppidrettsgymnas/NTG) in Bærum (near Oslo). ©2015 www.challenginglearning.com

QUESTION:
Should Bjørn move to France?

Alcohol is much cheaper in France than it is in Norway.

QUESTION:
Should Bjørn move to France?

Bjørn recently read the autobiography of a Tour de France winner. He wrote that the most significant thing he did as a young rider was to compete in the tough culture of the French professional road racing circuit.

QUESTION:
Should Bjørn move to France?

In mid-winter, daylight hours in the south of France are 9 hours, whereas in Oslo they are less than 6.

QUESTION:
Should Bjørn move to France?

Bjørn's father was recently diagnosed with lung cancer.

QUESTION:
Should Bjørn move to France?

Bjørn's father recently presented Bjørn with a scrapbook containing all of the newspaper clippings and pictures from when he had been a competitive cyclist.

QUESTION:
Should Bjørn move to France?

Bjørn's mother and father recently gave Bjørn a photograph that showed him as a toddler on his first bike. On the back his father had written: *"Carpe diem! Love, Mom and Dad."*

QUESTION:
Should Bjørn move to France?

Bjørn took part in the Gran Fondo Stelvio in Italy last June, but he really struggled with the unusually hot conditions.

QUESTION:
Should Bjørn move to France?

Bjørn struggles with juggling the demands of his full-time academic studies with his commitment to cycle training.

QUESTION:
Should Bjørn move to France?

Bjørn has been offered the chance to ride professionally for French cycle team FDJ.

QUESTION:
Should Bjørn move to France?

Bjørn currently lives at home with his parents and his fifteen-year-old younger brother.

QUESTION:
Should Bjørn move to France?

Bjørn is taking his girlfriend to Paris for a long weekend break to celebrate her birthday.

QUESTION:
Should Bjørn move to France?

Bjørn has told his girlfriend that he has something he needs to talk to her about.

QUESTION:
Should Bjørn move to France?

Bjørn recently took time to talk at length with his mother about his father's condition and to express gratitude to her for everything they had both done for him.

©2015 www.challenginglearning.com

QUESTION:
Should Bjørn move to France?

Bjørn's mother is named Marie-Christine.

©2015 www.challenginglearning.com

QUESTION:
Should Bjørn move to France?

You can win a gold medal at the Olympic Games for BMX and mountain biking.

©2015 www.challenginglearning.com

QUESTION:
Should Bjørn move to France?

Bjørn is studying Sports Science at a University in Oslo.

©2015 www.challenginglearning.com

QUESTION:
Should Bjørn move to France?

There hasn't been a French winner of the Tour de France since Bernard Hinault in 1985.

©2015 www.challenginglearning.com

QUESTION:
Should Bjørn move to France?

Bjørn's first bike was blue.

©2015 www.challenginglearning.com

QUESTION:
Should Bjørn move to France?

Bjørn Larsen is 20 years old.

QUESTION:
Should Bjørn move to France?

Bjørn currently receives coaching and financial support through the state-funded elite athlete development program.

► Figure 13: Bjørn Mystery (Set B)

QUESTION:
Should Bjørn move to France?

Direct budget airline routes from France to Norway fly only in the summer. A standard return ticket from Oslo to Paris can cost €350 in winter holiday months.

QUESTION:
Should Bjørn move to France?

Bjørn has enrolled on a beginner's French language course.

QUESTION:
Should Bjørn move to France?

Bjørn's biggest rival in the Norwegian young rider development program is the son of the senior coach.

QUESTION:
Should Bjørn move to France?

Bjørn's girlfriend drives a Citroën.

QUESTION:
Should Bjørn move to France?

Bjørn has no real fixed monthly outgoings at the moment. If he moved to France he would need to buy food and pay for transport. He would also become a French taxpayer.

QUESTION:
Should Bjørn move to France?

Bjørn doesn't know anyone in France, although there are other international young riders on the FDJ team.

QUESTION:
Should Bjørn move to France?

The FDJ cycle team would pay Bjørn a starting salary of €25,000 and would provide free accommodation for him.

QUESTION:
Should Bjørn move to France?

Bjørn would have a full-time commitment to the professional cycle team. Opportunities to return to Norway would be limited to just a few weeks each year and mainly in the winter months.

QUESTION:
Should Bjørn move to France?

Bjørn receives funding of €15,000 per year as part of the national elite athlete development program. This would be guaranteed for the next two years if he remains part of that program.

QUESTION:
Should Bjørn move to France?

Bjørn has never spent more than 3 weeks away from home before.

QUESTION: Should Bjørn move to France? **Bjørn's course tutor at University has been a professional skier, but his career was cut short through injury.** ©2015 www.challenginglearning.com	QUESTION: Should Bjørn move to France? **Bjørn enjoys meeting his friends in the evenings to play football or watch movies.** ©2015 www.challenginglearning.com

Deepening the Dialogue

Once your students have sorted through the first set of cards, you could prompt them to think a little more about the issues, asking them about one or more of the following:

- the definition of *life choices*
- types of life choices that people can be presented with
- choices and/or dilemmas that making choices generates
- personal opportunity and self-interest
- social interests
- opportunity and opportunism
- risk and reward of life choices
- aspiration and self-determination
- chance and good fortune in relation to life choices
- considerations of status, social and economic security in relation to life choices
- responsibilities that affect and are affected by our decision making
- consequences and implications of life choices
- sacrifices that people may make in relation to making a choice
- ethical and moral principle
- effects of personal life choices on others
- responsibility and life choices
- selflessness and life choices
- ambition and life choices
- risk versus reward

Facilitative Questions

The following questions should help you engage your students more deeply in the Bjørn Mystery. They can be used before, during or after your students have sifted through the

cards. Remember not to over-facilitate, though! Your students need time to talk with each other and deepen their own thinking.

1. How would you define a life choice?

2. *Carpe diem* is Latin. It is widely translated as "seize the day." What does this mean? Is this good advice?

3. Is making a life choice that takes advantage of an opportunity always a good thing?

4. If you won a free holiday of a lifetime but you knew you'd miss an important exam, miss a family reunion, let your sports team down, etc., what would you do then?

5. Are some opportunities just too good to miss?

6. What is the difference between making a life choice and opportunism?

7. What are the differences between making the most of opportunities that arise and being opportunistic?

8. In what ways do our life choices define our individual identity?

9. Are some people's ambitions never realized simply because people around them didn't support them?

10. Should we judge other people's ambition?

11. If someone's ambition is just to be famous, should we support that as much as if someone's ambition is to be a brain surgeon?

12. How much do personal strength, wealth and security contribute to an individual's ability to make life choices or to be in control of his or her own future?

13. Tennis player Serena Williams, Formula 1 driver Lewis Hamilton and footballer Lionel Messi are all people who have in various ways been described as single-minded and driven and who are said to have made sacrifices early in their careers. What do we mean by sacrifice? Do you think that other people had to make sacrifices for *them* too?

14. What's the difference between single-mindedness and selfishness?

15. Is selfishness an important and necessary part of being successful?

16. Can you still make life choices if your aim in life is to be selfless by always thinking of others first?

17. Is it possible to make a life choice in relation to an opportunity that emerges without its having a negative impact on someone else?

18. What is the relationship between the desire to be popular and the willingness to seize opportunities?

19. To what degree does making a life choice have to be a conscious act?

20. There is a saying that "You make your own luck in life." Is this true?

21. To be successful learners, we must learn to deal with challenge. Is this the same as making difficult life choices?

Next Steps

- -

Once your students have sorted the cards in groups and agreed on an answer to the question "Should Bjørn move to France?" you could ask each group to report back to the wider group. After that, or perhaps as part of the report-back session, you could also get your students to use an Opinion Line (see Section 7.2) to show their current thinking.

Opinion Line: Bjørn should move to France. (Agree or Disagree)

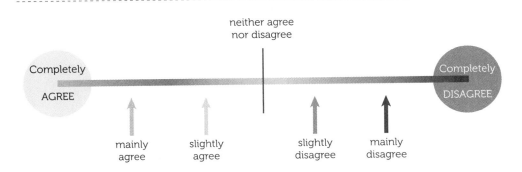

When your students have placed themselves along the imaginary line, ask them to explain to each other their reasoning.

Reviewing the Learning

Here are some questions to encourage your students to review the Bjørn Mystery:

- Is your answer significantly different from those of others in your group (or in another group)?
- If your answer was different from someone else's in your group, how did you reach a consensus?
- Have you thought about the implications that might present themselves when taking an opportunity?
- Can you think of three opportunities you've taken in life and any you've missed?
- Can you think of any opportunities that came out of nowhere?
- Can you think of opportunities that you've created for yourself through your own actions?
- Make a list of the two types.

8.9.2 • MYSTERY: LOUIS PASTEUR AND THE ANTHRAX VACCINE

By Steve Williams

This Mystery follows the reading of a script about Louis Pasteur's discovery of the anthrax vaccine. It imagines a group of young people who are interested in finding things out. However, what they find out comes from different perspectives or seems problematic. The groups talk about the problems. In this sense, the script is in the tradition of a written dialogue of ideas. It raises issues about causation, knowledge, fame, ethics and science.

My research for the script uncovered interesting information about a rival of Pasteur's called Max Von Pettenkofer, who rejected germ theory. I also found out that Pasteur was contracted by the Australian government in 1857 to wage biological warfare on the rabbit population. I have used this script with pupils aged ten and above with success.

The script is available in Appendix 2.

A Mystery About the Causes of Anthrax

- -

This Mystery about the causes of anthrax is suggested by the characters in the story in Part Three of the script (Appendix 2). You should allow the students to explore their own categories for the statements found therein. They will probably choose headings such as "likely causes," "not causes" or "possible causes." They need to rank the causes in order of the most influential or perhaps the first or last in the chain of causes.

▶ Figure 14: **Anthrax Mystery**

- -

QUESTION: What were the causes of anthrax in the sheep Pasteur studied on the farm?	QUESTION: What were the causes of anthrax in the sheep Pasteur studied on the farm?
Farmers buried diseased sheep in a field where there were live sheep. ©2015 www.challenginglearning.com	**The sheep were not healthy.** ©2015 www.challenginglearning.com
QUESTION: What were the causes of anthrax in the sheep Pasteur studied on the farm?	QUESTION: What were the causes of anthrax in the sheep Pasteur studied on the farm?
Pasteur injected some sheep with anthrax. ©2015 www.challenginglearning.com	**Sheep were not vaccinated.** ©2015 www.challenginglearning.com

QUESTION: What were the causes of anthrax in the sheep Pasteur studied on the farm?	QUESTION: What were the causes of anthrax in the sheep Pasteur studied on the farm?
Farmers didn't care for their sheep.	**Worms carried blood from dead animals to live ones.**
©2015 www.challenginglearning.com	©2015 www.challenginglearning.com
QUESTION: What were the causes of anthrax in the sheep Pasteur studied on the farm?	QUESTION: What were the causes of anthrax in the sheep Pasteur studied on the farm?
Sheep had cuts and scratches.	**Sheep arteries and veins got blocked.**
©2015 www.challenginglearning.com	©2015 www.challenginglearning.com
QUESTION: What were the causes of anthrax in the sheep Pasteur studied on the farm?	QUESTION: What were the causes of anthrax in the sheep Pasteur studied on the farm?
Anthrax was a killer disease.	**Worms ate dead animals.**
©2015 www.challenginglearning.com	©2015 www.challenginglearning.com

QUESTION: What were the causes of anthrax in the sheep Pasteur studied on the farm?	QUESTION: What were the causes of anthrax in the sheep Pasteur studied on the farm?
God wanted the animals to die.	Sheep were killed for humans to eat.
©2015 www.challenginglearning.com	©2015 www.challenginglearning.com
QUESTION: What were the causes of anthrax in the sheep Pasteur studied on the farm?	QUESTION: What were the causes of anthrax in the sheep Pasteur studied on the farm?
Sheep veins were not big enough.	Farmers lost money when sheep died.
©2015 www.challenginglearning.com	©2015 www.challenginglearning.com
QUESTION: What were the causes of anthrax in the sheep Pasteur studied on the farm?	QUESTION: What were the causes of anthrax in the sheep Pasteur studied on the farm?
Sheep ate infected grass.	Blood traveled around the bodies of the sheep.
©2015 www.challenginglearning.com	©2015 www.challenginglearning.com

8.9.3 • MYSTERY: IS SALLY A GOOD FRIEND?

By Jill Nottingham

I designed this Mystery to support and encourage six- to twelve-year-olds to inquire into the concept of friendship and what it means to be a good friend.

Friendship is an integral part of children's and adults' lives and comes in many different forms and interpretations. Parents and teachers encourage and implore children to "make friends" and be a "nice" or a "good" friend. Often, though, the children don't fully understand the concept. So this Mystery is one way to begin to deconstruct the concept of friendship and examine areas such as the nature of friendship (mutual caring, intimacy, shared activity) and the value and justification of friendship (its social and individual value) in order to reconstruct a new understanding and definition of what a friend is.

The information cards are provided in two separate sets. The first set contains the main body of information, and the second set provides additional information that might cause your students to re-evaluate their conclusion.

Using the Sally Mystery With Your Students

Age range: 6+

Key Words

Friends, friendship, friendliness, love, care, respect, honesty, sharing, time, social value, individual value, kindness, thoughtfulness, reciprocation, justification

Learning Intention

To investigate the concept of friendship

Success Criteria

To reach the learning goal, students will

- question the meaning and nature of friendship,

- inquire into different forms of friendship,

- challenge their own and each other's preconceptions and reasoning about what it is to be a friend,

- work toward creating a new individual and shared understanding and definition of friendship and friend.

Setting the Scene

Unlike the other two Mysteries shared in this chapter, the Sally Mystery probably needs no introduction. All you should need to do is split your students into groups of three or four and give each group the first set of cards shown in Figure 15. As the groups begin to sort through the cards, ask them to think about the question: Is Sally a good friend?

Avoid the temptation to give too many instructions to your students at this stage. Part of the intended challenge of this Mystery is that your students should think about how to solve the Mystery as well as what their answer might be. So let each group sort through the cards in whatever way they see fit. Do not take a lead or tell them how they should sort them. Of course, you might need to intervene if you think some students are being excluded by others or if someone is dominating, but otherwise, in the early stages of the activity, you should leave your students to find their own strategy.

Once they have sorted through the first set of cards, give them the second set shown in Figure 16. This should cause them to re-evaluate their early conclusions and lead to more dialogue.

▶ Figure 15: **Is Sally a Good Friend? (Set A)**

Jenny loves spending time in Sally's bedroom.

Sally always tries to use her manners.

Sally does jobs for her mom to earn spending money.

Sally has one older brother named Tim and a younger sister named Jenny.

Sally goes to sports club every Tuesday.

Sally has three best friends: Anna, Joe and Lucy.

ACTIVITY:
Is Sally a good friend?

Sally helps Jenny put her coat and shoes on in the morning.

©2015 www.challenginglearning.com

ACTIVITY:
Is Sally a good friend?

Sally is 7 years old.

©2015 www.challenginglearning.com

ACTIVITY:
Is Sally a good friend?

Sally loves cuddles with her cat Tigger.

©2015 www.challenginglearning.com

ACTIVITY:
Is Sally a good friend?

Sally loves to read and draw.

©2015 www.challenginglearning.com

ACTIVITY:
Is Sally a good friend?

Sally really likes her teacher, Mrs. Phillips.

©2015 www.challenginglearning.com

ACTIVITY:
Is Sally a good friend?

Tim thinks Sally is annoying.

©2015 www.challenginglearning.com

Figure 16: Is Sally a Good Friend? (Set B)

ACTIVITY:
Is Sally a good friend?

Lucy and Joe don't like each other very much.

©2015 www.challenginglearning.com

ACTIVITY:
Is Sally a good friend?

Mom gets upset with Sally for leaving her bedroom untidy.

©2015 www.challenginglearning.com

ACTIVITY:
Is Sally a good friend?

Sally's mom wishes Sally would listen to what she is told.

©2015 www.challenginglearning.com

ACTIVITY:
Is Sally a good friend?

Sally and Lucy both enjoy choosing which game to play at recess.

©2015 www.challenginglearning.com

ACTIVITY:
Is Sally a good friend?

Sally and Lucy had an argument this week.

©2015 www.challenginglearning.com

ACTIVITY:
Is Sally a good friend?

Sally gets grumpy if she is tired.

©2015 www.challenginglearning.com

Facilitative Questions

The following questions should help you engage your students more deeply in the Sally Mystery. They can be used before, during or after your students have sifted through the cards. Remember not to over-facilitate, though! Your students need time to talk with each other and deepen their own thinking.

Questions for Five- to Seven-Year-Olds

- What are friends?
- What do friends do?
- What don't friends do?
- How do you know if someone is your friend or not?
- Is it good to have lots of friends?
- Why should people try to be friends with each other?
- Do you always have to be nice to your friends?
- How is a good friend different from a friend?
- If a friend won't share food with you, does that mean this person is no longer your friend?
- Can you be friends with animals or objects?
- How many different types of friends can you have?

Questions for Seven- to Eleven-Year-Olds

- What is a good friend?
- Who is Sally a good friend to? Or not?
- What is the difference between a friend and a good friend?
- If you are not a good friend, does that mean you are not a friend at all?
- How is a good friend different from a best friend?
- To be a good friend, does that mean you *always* have to be friends with someone?
- How many different types of friends can you have? What are these types?
- Do friends have to be people?
- Are imaginary friends really friends?

Questions for Twelve- to Sixteen-Year-Olds

- What are the key ingredients of friendship?
- What is the connection between love and friendship?
- Can you be a friend but have no friends?
- Can unrequited friendship exist?
- In what sense is shared activity central to friendship?
- What justifies particular friendships?
- Can you be friends with yourself?
- Can you measure the depth of friendship by the amount of time invested in it?
- How well do you need to know someone before that person becomes a friend?
- Is it ever possible to know *everything* about another person?
- Can family be friends in their own right?

> "Reason is, and ought only to be, the slave of the passions and can never pretend to any other office than to serve and obey them."
>
> (David Hume, 1711–1776)

ODD ONE OUT

9.0 • PREVIEW

(Martin) *Odd One Out* is the first strategy I ever tried when I started trying to improve dialogue. I chose this because it was quick to design, simple to use with my students and easy to apply in any curriculum subject.

When I first tried it with a group of thirteen-year-old students in an English lesson, the overwhelming enthusiasm from the students to give answers, offer alternatives and go beyond the first, most obvious responses convinced me that this strategy was a powerful tool, not only for dialogue and thinking but also for inclusion and the development of core subject vocabulary.

Wherever the Odd One Out strategy is introduced, it provides a quick and ready stimulus to engage students and encourage them to sort characteristics, give reasons and develop the language of comparison and distinction.

In this chapter I share some ideas for Odd One Out that I have used with my twelve- to eighteen-year-old students, and Jill explains how she has used, adapted and extended Odd One Out to get the best from her younger learners.

It has been said that the simplest ideas are often the best ideas, and Odd One Out is certainly a testament to that notion. Give it a try with your students, and I'm sure you'll be more than satisfied with the results.

> By engaging students in comparing and contrasting, the Odd One Out strategy builds the language of sorting, classifying, identity and reason.

9.1 • ODD ONE OUT

The basic principle in Odd One Out is that you show your students three items, images, words or numbers. The students choose which one is different from the other two and give reasons for their selection. It's that simple!

For example, in primary mathematics, give your students the three numbers shown in Figure 17 and ask, "Which is the odd one out and why?"

▶ Figure 17: **Odd One Out With Three Numbers**

Here are some answers that your students might give:

Five (5) is the odd one out because it is the only:

- odd number
- prime number

Six (6) is the odd one out because it is the only:

- multiple of 3
- number that is not a multiple of 5

Ten (10) is the odd one out because it is the only:

- two-digit number
- number with a zero in the units column
- number that is not consecutive with the other numbers

As you can see, there are many different answers.

This activity should engage your students in thinking and in dialogue. It is inclusive because you can accept any of the three options as the correct answer (as long as your students can justify their choice with a valid reason). This will encourage your students to go beyond their first idea and to keep exploring further possibilities, often trying to find a more detailed or more obscure reason than their friends can!

Here is another example. Look at the three images in Figure 18, and decide which you think is the odd one out. Make sure you have a reason for your choice.

▶ Figure 18: **Odd One Out With a Hippo, Duck and Tiger**

Artwork by Katherine Renton (www.katherinerenton.com)

Now challenge yourself: Can you make each image the odd one out for a different reason?

9.2 • BENEFITS OF ODD ONE OUT

In the hippo, duck and tiger example shown in Figure 18, you should be able to think of lots of different odd one out answers. Your students should find the same thing. Indeed, because of the numbers of students you have, they should be able to come up with many more answers (and perhaps more obscure ones) than you can by yourself!

Wherever possible, capture your students' language by, for example, writing each response on a flipchart or whiteboard. A single word or short phrase will do to reflect the idea. If a student says, "The duck is the odd one out because it only has two legs and the others have four legs," then you can just write "two legs."

There are many advantages to recording your students' responses. In particular, it demonstrates the inclusive nature of the task when every idea gets equal billing. The shared vocabulary will also give your students ownership of the task, and in so doing give a sense of engagement and motivation.

Odd One Out also gives your students the opportunity to exercise their skills of sorting and classifying. These are fundamental thinking skills that all human beings use to help make sense of the world we live in. How is "this" the same as, or different from, "that"? This key question underpins the way we understand the world and puts language at the heart of expressing that understanding.

To ensure you get lots of good dialogue, a variety of ideas and an inclusive ethos when you design an Odd One Out for your students, try it yourself first, and make sure that *you* can give at least one reason (or, even better, two reasons) why *each* image could be the odd one out.

> The Odd One Out strategy is inclusive because it allows students to engage at a range of levels (from the obvious answers to the more obscure similarities and differences).

9.3 • HOW TO USE ODD ONE OUT EFFECTIVELY

The Odd One Out strategy is the perfect vehicle for using the Think-Pair-Share structure we shared with you in Section 7.1.

When you first show the three Odd One Out items, you should give your students a short time to think to themselves (Think). Then you can give them thirty to sixty seconds for paired dialogue (Pair). This will give them the opportunity to explore additional responses, ask each other questions, view things from a different perspective and practice the vocabulary they need to answer the question. Finally, you can ask your students to share their ideas with the whole group (Share).

As your students begin to add more and more ideas, you can stop the discussion and give them the chance to reflect for a further thirty seconds in pairs again. Ask them whether the ideas they have heard have prompted any new thoughts.

To build on this and to encourage deeper thinking, you could show a second Odd One Out set of three. This usually works best if they are linked to the first set. The second set can create a sense of re-energization, and you will probably notice that your students start their paired conversations at a higher level. For example, they might say things like, "That's too obvious. Is there something else we could say?" This is an explicit attempt to push their ideas beyond the first thought as well as a deliberate act to progress their thinking.

A third Odd One Out set is usually a good way to round off the activity, though you will probably find that the students have begun to exhaust possibilities at this stage. Keep the third set short, and record only one or two reasons for each image.

9.4 • WHY AND WHEN TO USE ODD ONE OUT

Odd One Out exercises should not be thought of as one-off starter activities. They can be used again and again to good effect.

As we have seen, there are a lot of benefits to using Odd One Out with your students. However, too many teachers use the approach a few times and then shelve it as a nice starter activity or a fun game rather than an integral part of learning. We believe this is a mistake.

That is not to say that an Odd One Out activity can't be used as a fun starter to engage the students in thinking. Your students might have spent the first hour of their day studying a Shakespeare play, then suffered an hour of long division in a math lesson before being drilled in grammar for another hour. Now you're supposed to be teaching them politics! Given all this, a fun starter activity would be no bad thing. It would also be a very good way to get your students' minds off all the other things they have been thinking about during the morning and onto something to do with politics.

For example, you could display three politicians and ask your students to identify the odd one out. Or three buildings connected to politics. Or three recent news headlines referring to contentious political decisions.

Furthermore, like any good learning activity, progression needs to be considered and planned to ensure that the rich vocabulary and engagement your students have shown are not lost.

(Martin) Recently I used photo versions of the hippo, duck and tiger cartoons in Figure 18 with a group of eight-year-olds. They were working on a science topic about birds and mammals. I showed them the three photos and asked them which is the odd one out and why. They thought about it, talked in pairs then shared their ideas with the whole group. I sat, marker pen in hand, ready to record their answers on a flipchart.

The first girl to respond said, "The duck is the odd one out because it has five feet." Stunned for a moment, I asked her to check her answer. Full of confidence, she stood up, pointed to the picture and counted the two feet on the duck, the two feet on the seagull behind it and the foot of a person who, in the photo version of the image, was *just* visible! Remembering the old adage "Never work with children and animals," I wrote on the flipchart paper, "feet."

Once the group was in full flow with their ideas, I then displayed a set of pictures showing a penguin, an eagle and a cow. They repeated their Think-Pair-Share and added more words to our list.

The students now had a collective vocabulary to explore the similarities and differences between birds and mammals. They took all the words they thought went with birds and put them in one column, then all the words to do with mammals went in another column. But there were some words that could go with both birds and mammals. The students had to decide what to do with these words, and this introduced them to the use of Venn diagrams. You can read more on the use of Venn diagrams as a thinking structure in Section 9.7.

In the next example, an art teacher was about to start a landscape project and wanted to encourage her fourteen- and fifteen-year-olds to design their own landscape image and continually improve it as they worked. Rather than telling the class what makes a good landscape, and how to paint it, the teacher showed three images (Figure 19) and asked the students, "Which is the odd one out and why?"

▶ **Figure 19: Artwork by Katherine Renton**
(www.katherinerenton.com)

These can be downloaded (for use with your students only) at challenginglearning.com.

The art teacher then wrote down all the ideas they came up with, noting phrases like *it has no buildings, it is cold, you can see the brushstrokes, it's a pencil drawing, uses darker tones, lighter background, more sky, the main subject is in the foreground* and so on.

The teacher then asked her students to choose three of their ideas that they thought would help them design the best still-life painting. They chose the following:

- You can see the brushstrokes.

- It has a building in the foreground.

- It uses darker tones in the background.

Throughout the project the teacher kept referring students back to their chosen criteria. With one student, the teacher looked at her work and asked why she'd used a bright sky for her painting when they had chosen to have darker tones as a criterion. The student explained that the building she was painting was made of dark stone and the detail was getting lost against the background, so she'd changed the background to make the building stand out more. The student was reasoning through the choices she had made against the criteria that had been selected in the Odd One Out activity.

> Here are some possible answers to the artwork Odd One Out.

9.5 • ODD ONE OUT VARIATIONS

In this section we look at some examples of how Odd One Out can be extended or adapted to increase the challenge for your students, pushing their thinking and reasoning skills.

Odd One Out Triangle

One way to extend the use of Odd One Out is to place the items in a triangle (as shown in Figure 20). This means your students can record the similarities along the sides and the differences at the points. Thus, if there is the similarity between 5 and 10 that they are both multiples of 5, then this points to the third number—in this case, 6—being the odd one out.

▶ Figure 20: **Odd One Out Triangle Example 1**

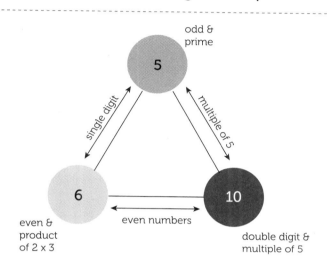

In the next example, students explore alternative visions of governance in the Spanish Civil War through the use of the Odd One Out. They are asked to record their answers on the triangle template shown in Figure 21.

▶ Figure 21: **Odd One Out Triangle Example 2**

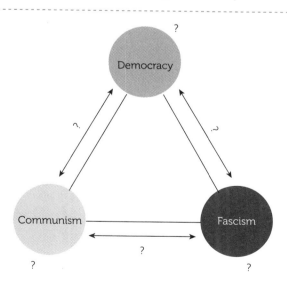

With the selection in Figure 21, it is not immediately obvious what to write at the points indicated by question marks. The beauty of this ambiguity is that it should encourage your students to clarify and analyze through dialogue with each other. Indeed, because the task is open-ended, your students will have the opportunity to clarify what is meant by the key terms and the relationships between them, as well as to decide which differences are the most significant.

> **Very often the three items you choose for an Odd One Out activity are of less importance than the dialogue that flows from that choice.**

Odd One Out Grid

Odd One Out activities do not necessarily need to be restricted to three concepts at a time, although this is an obvious choice to begin with. A grid such as the number grid shown in Figure 22 is a useful variation on the theme.

▶ Figure 22: **Odd One Out Grid**

	A	B	C
1	11	3	2
2	4	7	14
3	8	12	5

A grid can be used to extend the life span and challenge of the Odd One Out strategy.

This variation allows for many more options and combinations of possible odd ones out as your students can focus on rows, columns or diagonals. They can then use and extend the language, vocabulary and learning they have applied to the previous row, column or diagonal when moving on to the next one.

It also means that your students can choose to increase or decrease the amount of challenge by choosing a harder or an easier set of three. Alternatively, you can ask them to identify which row or column has the most possible answers. Accordingly, a grid such as this might offer more points of access for different abilities of students.

You can extend your students' thinking further with the use of additional questions such as these:

- Which column/row/diagonal has the most/least odd ones out?
- How many different categories of odd one out can we find (e.g., multiples, place value, number of digits, odd or even)?
- Are there any patterns to our answers?

As an additional challenge, rows or columns can be combined so that your students examine a larger quantity of numbers at one time. You can also begin with a blank grid and encourage the students to fill it themselves.

9.6 • ODD ONE OUT EXAMPLES

Math

Here are some other math examples:

- triangular prism, square-based pyramid, cuboid
- analog clock face, digital clock face, different type of analog clock
- decimals, fractions, percentages and whole numbers
- algebraic equations

▶ Figure 23: **Odd One Out: Properties of Materials**

Science

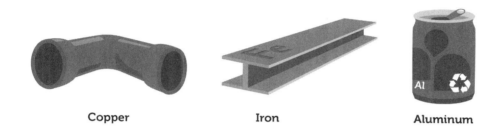

| Copper | Iron | Aluminum |

Answers should focus on properties of the different materials, including these:

- malleability
- melting point
- reactivity
- color
- use
- density
- corrosion
- strength

Here are some other science examples:

- oxygen, carbon dioxide, water vapor
- red blood cells, oxygen, platelets
- bronchiole, trachea, gullet
- whales, fish, shrimp
- different habitats
- different food nutrient groups
- solids, liquids, gases

▶ Figure 24: **Odd One Out: Shakespeare Plays**

Literacy

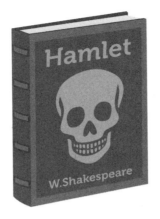 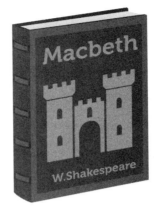 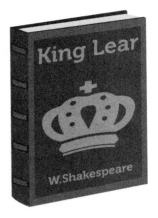

Answers could focus on the characters and/or the plays. For example:

- personalities of title characters
- nature of the play
- madness
- honor
- love
- family relationships
- setting
- endings
- leading female characters
- symbolism
- supernatural

Here are some other literacy examples:

a. Word-level work: **bounce, beautiful, baby**

Answers might focus on:

- nouns, adjectives, verbs, adverbs
- number of syllables
- beginning sounds
- end sounds
- silent letters

b. Sentence-level work:

Jenny raced quickly in the corridors.

Jenny ran fast down the wet corridor.

"Silly Jenny, stop running!"

Answers might focus on:

- use of punctuation

- sentence structure

- pronouns, nouns, verbs, adverbs, adjectives, etc.

- statements, instructions, explanations

c. Other examples

- comparing stories: "The Three Little Pigs," "Goldilocks and the Three Bears," "Little Red Riding Hood"

- comparing three different newspaper articles about a story on a similar theme

- comparing three different types of poem

Geography

- Norway, Sweden, Denmark

- London, Washington, Sydney

- sea, river, estuary

- earthquakes, storms, floods

- sustainable fuels

- seasons

History/Politics

- World War I, the Revolutionary War, the Battle of Waterloo

- Hitler, Stalin, Mussolini

- Florence Nightingale, Marie Curie, Mary Seacole

- John Adams, John Quincy Adams, Thomas Jefferson

- Henry VIII, Mary I, Elizabeth I

9.7 • EXTENDING ODD ONE OUT WITH VENN DIAGRAMS

In Section 9.4, Martin talked about how he used the hippo, duck and tiger (Figure 18) to help his students identify features of mammals and features of birds. Of course, there are a number of features that apply to both mammals and birds. For young students, this type of thinking is complex. One way to help them sort, classify and gain clarity in their thinking is through the use of a Venn diagram.

Venn diagrams are very effective extensions of the Odd One Out strategy.

▶ Figure 25: **Venn Diagram of Mammals and Birds**

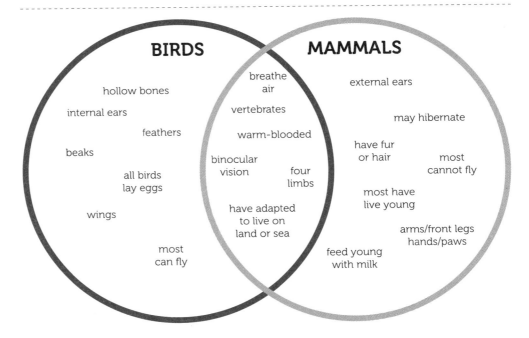

The diversity of life on Earth means that the classification of organisms is not straightforward, and the students' discussion can be made more complex by mentioning bats (mammals that can fly), penguins (birds that use their wings to swim) and of course the duck-billed platypus, which has a beak, lays eggs and has webbed feet but has no wings, is covered with fur and is classified as a mammal.

The use of a visual tool such as the Venn diagram shown in Figure 25 contributes to the engagement, depth and flow of dialogue. This is because Venn diagrams make thinking visible. They also help your students become more aware of their thought processes and show you how much they have understood key features of a concept or idea.

To begin with, you should pick two concepts that do not overlap with each other; for example, odd and even numbers. Draw two circles and ask your students to place the numbers from 1 to 20 into the correct hoop (Figure 26).

▶ Figure 26: **Venn Diagram With No Overlapping Concepts**

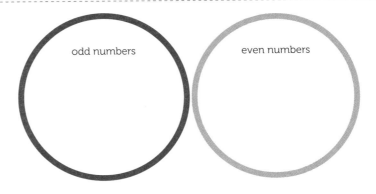

Now introduce your students to two overlapping concepts so that the Venn diagram circles need to overlap each other (Figure 27).

► Figure 27: **Venn Diagram With Overlapping Concepts**

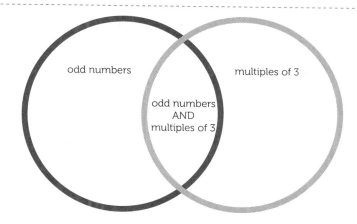

Remind students that numbers that are neither odd nor a multiple of 3 should go outside the diagram.

Returning to the Odd One Out examples we gave in Section 9.6, the Venn diagrams in Figure 28 (follows on from Figure 24), Figure 29 (follows on from Figure 23) and Figure 30 can be created from the answers given.

► Figure 28: **Venn Diagram of** *Hamlet, Macbeth* **and** *King Lear*

Also see Figure 24

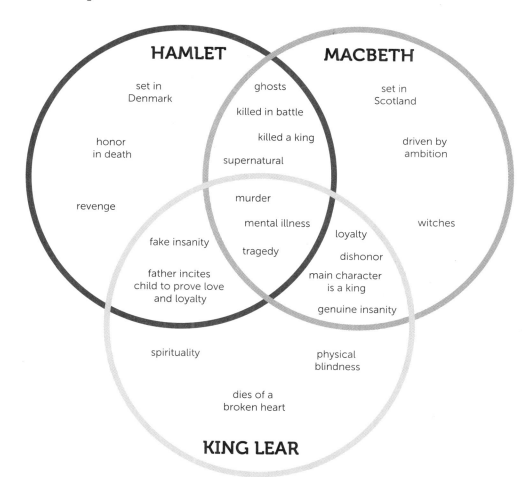

Also see Figure 23

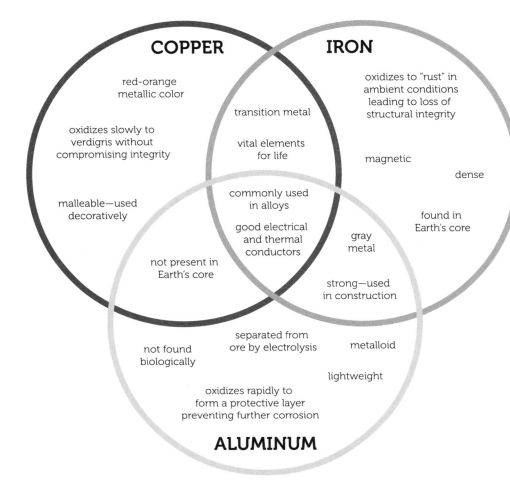

| 9. Odd One Out

▶ Figure 30: Venn Diagram of Geological Properties

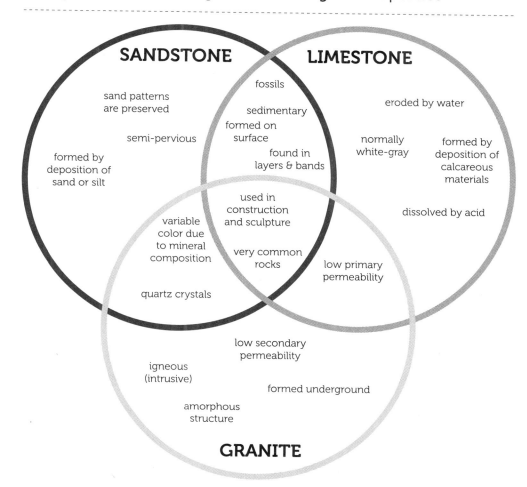

This chapter has shown you how to use the Odd One Out strategy. The key points included the following:

1. Odd One Out can be used in every area of the curriculum.

2. Odd One Out engages students in dialogue and provides a stimulus for comparing similarities and differences.

3. Odd One Out prompts students to engage in thinking about key subject concepts and key thinking skills such as quality, relation, importance and type.

4. By using Odd One Out strategies, your students will develop the shared language they need to make progress in, express and clarify their understanding.

Please note that the progress made by your students in this sort of activity is not just to do with subject matter, although that is of course important. Your students will also make progress by internalizing relevant concepts and questions. As their comprehension of the terms and the process increases, so too does their understanding of why general and specific concepts are crucial to thinking.

Following on from this, we suggest you encourage your students to look for other opportunities to compare concepts even when not using the Odd One Out strategy. These are the sorts of questions they can ask themselves:

1. In what ways are these things the *same*?

2. What *qualities* are the *same*?

3. What are the most *important similarities*?

4. Are the things *different* in more ways than they are the *same*?

5. Can we *measure* the *qualities* of *sameness* or *difference*?

6. How do we come to know of the qualities the things share—by *observation*, *assumption* or *inference*?

You can also use these questions to prompt students both within and outside of Odd One Out exercises.

Like other strategies for engaging your students in dialogue, Odd One Out can support the learning of key thinking words. In the examples given in this chapter, these include:

- subject-specific concepts such as communism, fascism, birds, mammals, odd number and prime number;

- thinking concepts such as compare, similar, related, type and category.

9.9 • NEXT STEPS AND FURTHER READING

Here are some suggestions for what you could do next so that you get the most out of this chapter:

1. Try a few different Odd One Out strategies with your students.

2. Encourage your students to find as many different answers to one set of three as they can.

3. Ask your students to create their own sets to think through and to challenge others with.

4. Use the sequence for small-group activities (Section 5.6) for an Odd One Out.

5. Add the strategies from this section to your Repertoire and Judgment Notes at the back of this book.

Based on a survey of thousands of comparisons between experimental and control groups, using a wide variety of subject areas, Robert Marzano identified nine categories of instructional strategies that improve student achievement:

1. Identifying similarities and differences

2. Summarizing and note-taking

3. Reinforcing effort and providing recognition

4. Homework and practice

5. Representing knowledge

6. Learning groups

7. Setting objectives and providing feedback

8. Generating and testing hypotheses

9. Cues, questions and advance organizers

You can read more about this in *Classroom Instruction That Works: Research-Based Strategies for Increasing Student Achievement* (Marzano, 2001).

> "I can prove anything by statistics except the truth."
>
> (George Canning, 1770–1827)

FORTUNE LINES

10.0 • PREVIEW

Similar to the Mystery strategy we looked at in Chapter 8, Fortune Lines give students evidence to evaluate and analyze. As with the Mystery, the activity challenges students to make decisions about the importance and relevance of the information before them and apply reasoning to the conclusions they draw. How your students link together the information and what they infer from it will provide an ideal opportunity for dialogue.

Unlike a Mystery, however, a Fortune Line requires students to interpret a chain of events *and* link them to a wider range of variables represented by the axes of a graph. In this way, the focus of Fortune Line activities is to explore two aspects of the information at the same time. This is typically emotions, fortunes or experiences on one axis and time or chronology on the other.

Your students will need to exercise their interpretation skills, check and refine their thinking and connect abstract data to evidence and events. For that reason, dialogue is essential if your students are going to be able to make sense of the information.

The key learning in the task is the process of reasoning and justification. It should also encourage your students' sense of inquiry and prompt them to undertake further research.

This chapter includes some examples of Fortune Lines to illustrate how they might be used.

> Fortune Lines engage students in dialogue about the fortunes of a main character.

> Fortune Lines are designed to blur the edges of fact and opinion, and to raise questions about the validity of assumptions and opinions.

10.1 • FORTUNE LINES

The x-axis of a Fortune Line always relates to time. The y-axis always relates to emotions, fortunes or experiences.

A Fortune Line is presented with a set of information broken down into chunks and given to the students on separate cards. The activity usually centers on one or more key (fictional or nonfictional) characters. Collaborative group work is an essential part of the activity, and it is the opinions and reasons generated during discussion that are important. There should always be some less relevant or ambiguous information included in the cards to allow for discussion.

Like any normal graph, Fortune Lines are open to interpretation; they give a big picture, from which the reader can draw conclusions. The main difference, though, between Fortune Lines and "normal" graphs is that Fortune Line axes are left deliberately vague so as to add further challenge to the idea of interpreting events.

Fortune Lines are accompanied by a set of cards, each with a key event shown on it. The students' task is to identify where on the Fortune Line each event should be placed.

For example, rather than listing the months of the year on the x-axis as with a normal graph, a Fortune Line might instead just say "Time." This means that the Fortune Line could be representing a week, a year, a decade or a century—or indeed any length of time. It is for the students to decide as they interpret the story.

Each Fortune Line will have a set of key events printed onto cards. Your students should take each event in turn and place it in the position on the graph that they think is most appropriate. This will then help your students create a narrative about the main character. Note that, as with Mysteries, Fortune Lines will always have ambiguous or purposefully misleading information included among the event cards. This is meant to encourage more thinking, questioning and deliberation.

10.2 • USING FORTUNE LINES

Divide your students into small groups. Give them the Fortune Line first and then give them the associated set of statements.

Ask them to do the following:

Once students have placed all the event cards on the Fortune Line, they should develop a narrative to tell the graph's story.

- Analyze the pattern of information presented by the graph.
- Decide which of the statements or scenarios helps explain the pattern of information on the graph, and indicate which part of the graph it helps explain.
- Place the statements on the graph to show where you think they best fit.
- Develop a narrative of events that explains the graph.

Please note that in some circumstances, you should give your students a blank Fortune Line and ask them to create the line(s) as they interpret the information. This is how it works with the Henry VIII Fortune Line in Section 10.3.

As your students are working, it is useful for them to see how other groups are interpreting their graphs. Use the jigsaw technique in Section 7.6 to encourage your students to justify their graphs to each other before returning to their home groups. In the home group, they can then change their minds, add to their own thinking or reinterpret the information in another way.

To increase the challenge, change a variable in the graph by, for example, stating that the time frame (on the x-axis) is ten years. Now that they know that, does it change the way they interpreted the statements?

10.3 • FORTUNE LINE OF HENRY VIII

By Joanne Nugent

This Fortune Line prompts questions about the actions, feelings and personal and political motivations of England's most notorious king, Henry VIII.

Your students will be prompted to investigate the fortunes of Henry VIII while considering the impact of factors such as other key characters of the period, the impact of decision making, the line of succession, gender equality, religion, egotism, greed and wealth.

Give your students an enlarged version of the blank graph shown in Figure 31. Ask them to organize the information (see the cards provided in Figure 32) chronologically and to question what it means to be happy from their own perspective and from that of Henry VIII. They should also consider what impact his happiness had on the lives of others.

Working in groups, your students should organize the information into categories. Here are some suggestions:

- the Reformation
- the break from Rome
- Henry VIII's six wives
- Act of Succession
- Act of Supremacy

Your students could also construct an Agree or Disagree chart to help them sort out the evidence that shows Henry VIII was happy from the evidence that shows he was not.

You can make the Fortune Line more active by getting your students to create a more physical Fortune Line in a large open space and move the cards around according to where they feel they should go. Students could also become the characters and move themselves up and down the fortune axis.

Key questions to consider:

1. What is happiness?
2. How important is it to be happy?
3. What makes someone happy?
4. What is equality?
5. To what extent does happiness affect our ability to make decisions?
6. What is the connection between love and happiness?
7. What is the connection between power and happiness?
8. Which pieces of information are irrelevant?

> The information that accompanies each Fortune Line should be incomplete so that students are prompted to raise questions and offer hypotheses.

▶ Figure 31: **Fortune Line: Was Henry VIII a Happy Monarch?**

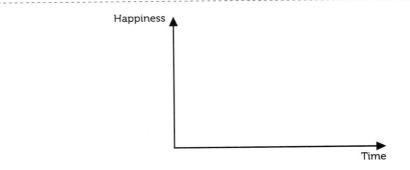

Happiness

Time

▶ Figure 32: **Cards to Go With the Fortune Line of Henry VIII**

1	Happiness is a mental or emotional state of well-being characterized by positive or pleasant emotions ranging from contentment to intense joy. ©2015 www.challenginglearning.com
2	28th June 1491 - Henry VIII is born. ©2015 www.challenginglearning.com
3	14th November 1501 - Henry's big brother Prince Arthur marries a Spanish princess known as Catherine of Aragon. ©2015 www.challenginglearning.com
4	2nd April 1502 - Prince Arthur dies age 15. ©2015 www.challenginglearning.com
5	Papal dispensation is given so that Henry VIII can marry his late brother's wife Catherine of Aragon. The marriage takes place on 11th June 1509. ©2015 www.challenginglearning.com
6	21st April 1509 - Henry VII dies. Henry VIII becomes King of England age 17. ©2015 www.challenginglearning.com
7	18th February 1516 - Catherine of Aragon gives birth to a daughter named Mary. ©2015 www.challenginglearning.com
8	4th March 1526 - Mary Boleyn gives birth to a son named Henry. Mary was Henry VIII's mistress, and her son was widely believed to be the King's child and longed-for son. ©2015 www.challenginglearning.com
9	Henry falls madly in love with Anne Boleyn. Many believe that he is obsessed with the young woman and desperate to make her his wife. ©2015 www.challenginglearning.com
10	Henry is desperate for a legitimate male heir to continue the Tudor line of succession. He has grown tired of Catherine of Aragon and her inability to give him a son. She did give birth to three sons, but not one survived. ©2015 www.challenginglearning.com

11	Henry believes his marriage to Catherine was wrong and he should never have been made to marry his late brother's wife. He believes God is unhappy with him. Henry annuls his marriage to Catherine in 1527. ©2015 www.challenginglearning.com
12	In 1529 Henry dismisses his chief advisor Chancellor Wolsey because he failed to convince the Pope to grant his divorce from Catherine of Aragon. ©2015 www.challenginglearning.com
13	1534 - Henry declares himself as Head of the Church of England. This is called the Act of Supremacy. ©2015 www.challenginglearning.com
14	3rd January 1533 - Henry marries Anne Boleyn. ©2015 www.challenginglearning.com
15	25th January 1533 - Henry is excommunicated by Pope Clement VII. ©2015 www.challenginglearning.com
16	31st May 1533 - Anne Boleyn is crowned Queen. ©2015 www.challenginglearning.com
17	7th September 1533 - Anne Boleyn gives birth to a daughter named Elizabeth. ©2015 www.challenginglearning.com
18	Divorce was against the rules of the Catholic Church. Henry had broken the rules. ©2015 www.challenginglearning.com
19	Henry loved playing tennis. He was an accomplished archer. He adored horse riding and jousting. ©2015 www.challenginglearning.com
20	1535 - Bishop John Fisher and Chancellor Thomas More are executed for refusing to acknowledge Henry as Head of the English Church. ©2015 www.challenginglearning.com
21	7th January 1536 - Catherine of Aragon dies. ©2015 www.challenginglearning.com
22	15th May 1536 - Anne Boleyn is tried for treason, adultery and incest at the Tower of London. ©2015 www.challenginglearning.com
23	19th May 1536 - Anne Boleyn is executed. ©2015 www.challenginglearning.com
24	30th May 1536 - Henry VIII marries Jane Seymour. ©2015 www.challenginglearning.com

25	12th October 1537 - Jane Seymour gives birth to a prince called Edward. He is Henry VIII's only legitimate male heir. ©2015 www.challenginglearning.com
26	24th October 1537 - Jane Seymour dies following complications of childbirth. ©2015 www.challenginglearning.com
27	6th January 1540 - Henry marries Anne of Cleves. ©2015 www.challenginglearning.com
28	9th July 1540 - Henry annuls his marriage to Anne of Cleves. He does not find her attractive and says she has a foul odor. ©2015 www.challenginglearning.com
29	28th July 1540 - Thomas Cromwell is executed for treason and heresy. Henry blames him for his marriage to Anne of Cleves. Cromwell was Henry's chief adviser. ©2015 www.challenginglearning.com
30	28th July 1540 - Henry VIII marries Catherine Howard. Catherine is 19 and Henry 49 years old. Henry adores Catherine and calls her his "rose without thorns." ©2015 www.challenginglearning.com
31	13th February - Catherine Howard is executed on the grounds of adultery. ©2015 www.challenginglearning.com
32	12th July 1543 - Henry VIII marries Catherine Parr. ©2015 www.challenginglearning.com
33	28th January - King Henry VIII dies age 57. ©2015 www.challenginglearning.com
34	1532 - Hans Holbein, a German artist, is appointed the King's painter. His paintings of the Tudor period have become iconic. ©2015 www.challenginglearning.com
35	A widely believed (but completely unproven) legend is that King Henry VIII composed the song "Greensleeves" for his lover and future queen consort Anne Boleyn. ©2015 www.challenginglearning.com
36	Many people said Anne Boleyn was a witch and had an extra finger. ©2015 www.challenginglearning.com
37	Henry gave permission for the Bible to be translated into English in 1537. Despite a break with Rome, England did not fully embrace Protestantism until Edward VI ascended to the throne. ©2015 www.challenginglearning.com
38	1536 - the "Dissolution of the Monasteries" began. The wealth and riches of the Catholic Church in England were passed directly to the Crown. ©2015 www.challenginglearning.com

39	The Third Succession Act of Henry VIII's reign was passed in July 1543, and returned both Mary and Elizabeth to the line of the succession behind their half-brother Edward.
	©2015 www.challenginglearning.com
40	The Succession to the Crown Act 2013 ended succession to the crown of England based upon gender. This means that if a girl is the firstborn child to a monarch she is the rightful heir to the crown.
	©2015 www.challenginglearning.com

Notes to Accompany the Henry VIII Fortune Line

Age range: 13+

Key Words

Happiness, guilt, love, politics, religion, reformation, renaissance, legitimacy, honesty, justification, ambiguity, empathy, spirituality, manipulation, power, conscience, Catholicism, Protestantism, succession, gender equality, chronology

Learning Intention

To question the actions of England's most notorious king

Success Criteria

To reach the learning goal, students will

- be able to outline the timeline of events in the Tudor period, 1491–1547;

- understand the role of key individuals and how they changed the course of history;

- identify the background and trigger factors behind Henry's actions;

- analyze the impact of decision making;

- assess whether personal or political motivation was behind the decision making of Henry VIII;

- challenge interpretations and compare results;

- use skills of inquiry to form a historical argument.

Facilitative Questions

The following questions should help you engage your students more deeply in the Henry VIII Fortune Line. They can be used before, during or after your students have sifted through the cards. Remember not to over-facilitate, though! Your students need time to talk with each other and deepen their own thinking.

1. What is happiness?

2. Should every monarch be happy?

3. What reasons would a ruler have for not being happy?

4. How can you tell that a person is happy?

5. Do you make better decisions when you are happy?

6. Can you make yourself happy?

7. Do people or possessions make you happy?

8. Is it pointless to pursue happiness?

9. Can happiness last forever?

10. Is happiness a momentary emotion?

11. Would you be happy to become king at age 17?

12. Can power make you happy?

13. Was Henry VIII spoiled?

14. Did Henry like himself?

15. Catherine of Aragon was a loyal and much loved Queen of England. Do you think Henry loved her?

16. Whom do you think Henry loved?

17. Is it important for a king and queen to love each other?

18. Why did Henry marry Anne Boleyn?

19. Why did Henry betray Anne and send her to the Tower?

20. What qualities do you think Henry most valued in others?

21. Why was Henry not content with his two healthy daughters?

22. Was Henry wrong to desire a son?

23. Was Henry wrong to pursue his dream of securing the Tudor dynasty?

24. Is there a difference between contentment and happiness?

25. Were Henry's queens happy?

26. Without the Reformation, would Catherine of Aragon have remained Queen of England and Anne Boleyn kept her head?

27. If Catherine of Aragon had had a healthy boy, would England have remained with Rome?

28. What were the reasons for Henry making himself head of the Church of England?

29. Henry was regarded as intelligent and cultured. Do you think this was the case? How do you judge a person as intelligent?

30. Was there benefit for Henry in the dissolution of the monasteries?

31. Was Henry responsible for the executions of Anne Boleyn and her cousin Catherine Howard?

32. Is it important that Henry never fully converted to Protestantism?

33. Hans Holbein's paintings have become iconic representations of the Tudor period. Is it wrong to judge an individual through the eyes of an artist?

34. Consider the idea of to what extent Henry VIII was happy.

35. Is there ever a simple yes/no answer in history?

36. Even if you were present at the event, would you know "the truth" about that event?

Varying the Challenge

If you need to increase or decrease the amount of challenge to cater for your students' varying needs, then you could do one or more of the following:

1. Remove some of the irrelevant cards.

2. Group the cards ready for your students. This could be around central themes such as the Reformation or line of succession.

3. Add cards that reflect the perspective of others from the period, for example, Henry's wives, Thomas More and so on.

4. Encourage your students to focus on the ambiguous pieces of information, and ask them to put together a case in support of the proposition that we can never really know the happiness of a person, particularly when related to a historical character.

   - Include copies of Hans Holbein's portraits of Henry VIII and his wives Jane Seymour and Anne of Cleves.

   - Or include his portraits of Catherine of Aragon, Anne Boleyn, Catherine Howard and Catherine Parr.

   - You could play the music "Greensleeves" as background music when your students are engaging in the task.

10.4 • FORTUNE LINE FOR A VISIT TO GRANDMA'S

(Jill) I created this Fortune Line to support a class of seven- and eight-year-olds in recognizing the features and structure of *recount* writing. This built on a previous lesson in which the children created a character sketch for the role of narrator.

I began by sharing the following text and then encouraged the children to identify the key features of the text: How does it begin? What tense is used? What is the importance of chronology, added details and the use of temporal connectives such as before, after, straightaway, later on and so on?

A Visit to Grandma's

It was a cold and windy Saturday when my friend Kelly and I decided to visit my grandma in York. We had been waiting at the bus station in the cold for twenty minutes when the bus finally came, and we were so pleased to get into the warmth.

The journey was quite long, but Kelly and I ate some fruit and talked all the way. To keep from getting too bored, we played a game where she tried to spot red cars and I tried to spot blue cars, and the one who had spotted the most cars when we got to York was the winner. Kelly won because more red cars passed us than blue cars.

After we got off the bus, we walked to my grandma's house. It was raining in York. And I was tired.

I was so excited to get to see her again, because she had always spoiled me with hugs and yummy treats when I went to visit her.

We finally arrived at Grandma's house five minutes later and she had cheese sandwiches and glasses of milk ready for us. We were so pleased because the journey had made us hungry. We ate the sandwiches and drank the milk; then I gave Grandma a great big hug and told her how much I loved her.

It had been a long journey and I was tired, but it was worth it to see Grandma again.

I then gave the children an enlarged copy of Figure 33, together with a copy of the recount text shown above. For the children who needed more support, I gave them the cards shown in Figure 34 instead as these have the same information but delivered in more manageable chunks.

I encouraged the children to annotate their graph with their reasons for why they feel the cards or text should be in those places. I also suggested that they could add their own adjectives or adverbs to support or describe the characters' feelings at that point.

Once the children had analyzed and identified the narrator's emotions at different points on the line, they then used the Fortune Line as inspiration for their subsequent recount writing. What emerged was greater detail about the narrator's feelings and emotions in the children's writing.

To extend this activity further, you could get your students to plot another line on the same graph to represent the perspective of Kelly or Grandma. This would draw attention to different perspectives of the same events.

▶ Figure 33: **Fortune Line for a Visit to Grandma's**

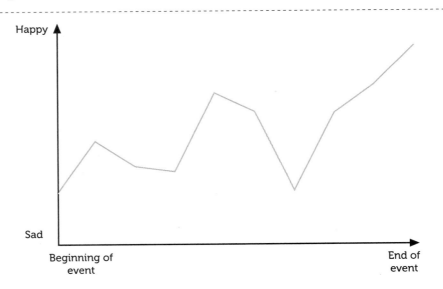

▶ Figure 34: **Cards to Go With the Fortune Line
for a Visit to Grandma's**

Set A

©2015 www.challenginglearning.com Kelly and I stood in the cold bus station.	©2015 www.challenginglearning.com The bus finally came.	©2015 www.challenginglearning.com It was a long journey.
©2015 www.challenginglearning.com Kelly and I ate some fruit.	©2015 www.challenginglearning.com Kelly and I played a game.	©2015 www.challenginglearning.com Kelly won the game.
©2015 www.challenginglearning.com We walked to Grandma's house.	©2015 www.challenginglearning.com We arrived at Grandma's house.	©2015 www.challenginglearning.com We ate sandwiches and drank milk.
©2015 www.challenginglearning.com I gave Grandma a big hug.		

Set B (Alternative Cards)

©2015 www.challenginglearning.com It was a cold and windy Saturday.	©2015 www.challenginglearning.com I met my friend Kelly.	©2015 www.challenginglearning.com Kelly and I stood in the chilly bus station.
©2015 www.challenginglearning.com We waited 20 minutes.	©2015 www.challenginglearning.com The bus finally came.	©2015 www.challenginglearning.com We climbed onboard the warm bus.
©2015 www.challenginglearning.com It was a long journey.	©2015 www.challenginglearning.com Kelly and I ate some fruit.	©2015 www.challenginglearning.com We talked all the way.
©2015 www.challenginglearning.com We tried not to get too bored.	©2015 www.challenginglearning.com Kelly and I played a game.	©2015 www.challenginglearning.com I spotted red cars.
©2015 www.challenginglearning.com Kelly spotted blue cars.	©2015 www.challenginglearning.com Kelly won the game.	©2015 www.challenginglearning.com We got off the bus.
©2015 www.challenginglearning.com We walked to Grandma's house.	©2015 www.challenginglearning.com It was raining in York.	©2015 www.challenginglearning.com I was so excited to see Grandma again.
©2015 www.challenginglearning.com We arrived at Grandma's house.	©2015 www.challenginglearning.com We ate cheese sandwiches and drank milk.	©2015 www.challenginglearning.com Grandma and I hugged tightly.
©2015 www.challenginglearning.com It told Grandma how much I loved her.	©2015 www.challenginglearning.com It had been a long journey.	©2015 www.challenginglearning.com It was all worth it to see Grandma again.

10.5 • REVIEW

This chapter has shown you how to use the Fortune Line strategy. The key points have included the following:

1. A Fortune Line is presented with a set of related statements. Your students should position the statements on the graph and give reasons to justify their interpretation.

2. Fortune Lines focus on emotions over time.

3. Fortune Lines invite speculation, explanation, reasoning and thinking about degrees of significance.

4. These are some key elements of Fortune Lines:

   - comparing one variable against another

   - comparing and predicting events

   - decision making

   - analyzing evidence

   - drawing on, and developing, subject knowledge and understanding

   - information processing

10.6 • NEXT STEPS AND FURTHER READING

Here are some suggestions for what you could do next so that you get the most out of this chapter:

1. Try out one of the Fortune Lines in this chapter with your students.

2. Encourage your students to find alternative positions for each of the cards.

3. Ask your students to create a set of questions generated from their dialogue about one of the Fortune Lines in this chapter.

4. Add the strategies from this section to your Repertoire and Judgment Notes at the back of this book.

5. Create a new Fortune Line to use with your students.

Fortune Lines are introduced and used extensively in a series of books edited by David Leat:

- Baumfield, V., & Leat, D. (Eds.). (2002). *Thinking through religious education.* Cambridge, UK: Chris Kington.

- Fisher, P., Wilkinson, I., & Leat, D. (Eds.). (2000). *Thinking through history.* Cambridge, UK: Chris Kington.

- Harbottle, C., Barlow, G., & Leat, D. (Eds.). (2007). *Thinking through PSHE.* Cambridge, UK: Chris Kington.

- Higgins, S., Baumfield, V., & Leat, D. (Eds.). (2000). *Thinking through primary teaching.* Cambridge, UK: Chris Kington.

- Leat, D. (2001). *Thinking through geography* (2nd ed.). Cambridge, UK: Chris Kington.

- Wright, D., Taverner, S., & Leat, D. (Eds.). (2009). *Thinking through mathematics.* Cambridge, UK: Chris Kington.

> "The aim of a thinking skills programme such as P4C is not to turn children into philosophers but to help them become more thoughtful, more reflective, more considerate and more reasonable individuals."
>
> (Lipman, 1991)

PHILOSOPHY FOR CHILDREN (P4C)

11

11.0 • PREVIEW

All the authors of this book wholeheartedly recommend the practice of Philosophy for Children. Indeed, it was this process that led to the founding of Challenging Learning (the company as well as the books).

P4C was developed by Matthew Lipman and his colleagues at the Institute for the Advancement of Philosophical Inquiry with Children. Lipman's intention was to emphasize many of the values of philosophy—wisdom, reflection, reasoning and reasonableness—and to ensure that they were part of every child's education. Since its inception in 1972, P4C has been developed in more than sixty countries worldwide, has been well researched, and proved to be an extremely positive approach to teaching and learning.

In our opinion, P4C offers the best set of strategies for developing the art of good thinking and dialogue with students. This chapter explains how it can be done.

P4C offers an excellent set of strategies for developing the art of good dialogue.

P4C focuses dialogue on a philosophical question. In doing so, it builds higher-order thinking, questioning, speaking and listening skills.

11.1 • PHILOSOPHY FOR CHILDREN

The fundamentals of Philosophy for Children are straightforward. Children, or older students, share some reading, listening or viewing with their teacher. The students take some thinking time to devise their own questions. They choose a question that interests them and, with the teacher's help, discuss it together. The teacher is concerned with getting students to welcome the diversity of each other's initial views and to use those as the start of a process that involves the students questioning assumptions, developing opinions with supporting reasons, analyzing significant concepts and applying the best reasoning and judgment they are capable of to the question they have chosen.

In the longer term, the teacher aims to build the students' skills and concepts through appropriate follow-up activities, thinking games and the orchestration of connections between philosophical discussions, life and the rest of the school curriculum.

11.2 • THE COMMUNITY OF INQUIRY

A central concept of P4C is that of the community of inquiry. This can be defined as a reflective approach to dialogue built up over time with a single group of students. The community embodies cooperation, care, respect and safety; the inquiry reaches for understanding, meaning, truth and values supported by reasons.

As a community of inquiry develops over time, participants' questions get deeper and more thoughtful. Their discussions are disciplined and focused yet, at the same time, imaginative. They care about what others say but don't accept easy answers. A community of inquiry combines critical, creative, caring and collaborative thinking.

11.3 • PHILOSOPHICAL QUESTIONS

A question to start a philosophical dialogue will contain, or at least imply, a concept from life and learning that is both important and questionable. It will also be an open question in the sense that it will not be asked from a position of authority with a preconceived answer in mind.

A starting question may have a "yes" or "no" answer and still be regarded as an open question because the answer begins a process of discussion rather than ending it. Hence, the following questions are open, and each has a philosophical dimension.

- Is graffiti art or vandalism?
- Can fair trade ever be possible?
- Can it ever be right to invade another country?
- Are extremes of wealth unjust? If so, should there be rules about maximum and minimum levels of wealth?
- Whom should I respect and why?
- Do I have more than one culture?
- If one person in a group misbehaves, is it always wrong to punish the whole group?

- Should scientists decide what societies should do about global warming because they are more knowledgeable about global warming than non-scientists?

- Is democracy always the best form of government?

- Is tolerance a virtue?

- What makes something or someone believable?

- Is it always good to be brave?

- What's the difference between real and make-believe?

You can help your students recognize open questions with philosophical dimensions. You can also help them create their own questions. We share some strategies for doing this later in the chapter.

11.4 • DIALOGUE THROUGH P4C

Dialogue in P4C starts with a shared stimulus. By that we mean you and your students share a story, look at an image, listen to a piece of music or engage in a piece of drama.

Together, you should then identify points of interest and significance. For example, your students might talk about what strikes them most about a painting, or they might identify the key concepts in a story. These ideas should then be shared and analyzed by the whole group.

> P4C begins with something that stimulates wonder (e.g., a story, an image or a piece of drama).

From these thoughts, you can encourage your students to ask philosophical questions. Normally this is done in small groups before sharing with the whole group. Think-Pair-Share (see Section 7.1) is an ideal structure for this.

Using a suitable voting method, your students should choose the best question. This question will then be the focus for the inquiry.

The inquiry proceeds according to the ground rules negotiated and regularly re-evaluated by your students (see Sections 2.6.4 and 5.2).

You should ensure that the dialogue continues in the spirit of a community of inquiry (see the next item). At the end, make time for individual reflections on the content and process of the dialogue.

These tried-and-tested routines provide a helpful structure with which to navigate the difficulties of classroom dialogue. Even so, the routines should not be seen as ends in themselves but always as the means to achieving a community of inquiry.

11.5 • P4C SEQUENCE—OVERVIEW

The following steps are guidelines only. You should adapt them—or even leave some of the steps out—if you think that would suit the context better.

> There are many ways to run a P4C dialogue. Here are some of the most common steps.

1. **Prepare**. Sit in a circle so everyone can see and hear one another. Give guidelines of conduct (these are always able to be reviewed by the group). You could use the suggestions in Section 5.2.

2. **Share a stimulus**. Present the stimulus to your students. The stimulus might be a narrative, a news item, a selection of contrasting arguments or explanations, a picture, a video, a work of art—anything that stimulates your students' thinking and prompts them to raise interesting ideas and questions.

3. **Identify issues and concepts**. Give time for individual reflection on the stimulus—maybe a minute of silent thinking or jotting down key words. Ask your students to share with a partner their thoughts about the issues raised. Write on the board their key words and some of their thoughts about what they thought was important or interesting about the stimulus.

4. **Create questions**. Split your students into small groups to generate open-ended, philosophical questions. When they have created a few, ask each group to choose their best one to present to the whole class.

5. **Choose and air questions**. Invite authors to explain or clarify their questions. Ask your other students to link, appreciate or evaluate any of the questions aired. Then get all your students to vote for what they consider to be the best question from the list you have collected from the groups. One way to encourage them to pick the "best" one rather than simply their favorite one is to say, "Pick the one you think will give us the best chance of an open-ended, philosophical discussion."

6. **Dialogue: First thoughts**. Once the best question has been selected, ask the authors of that question to open the dialogue by sharing their initial thoughts—perhaps their expectations of where the question might lead or the answers they currently have in mind.

7. **Dialogue: Build and challenge**. Bring other students into the dialogue by inviting comments, responses, examples, agreements, disagreements, reasons and so on. You might need to introduce other relevant perspectives or possible arguments if the dialogue is too limited in scope.

8. **Dialogue: Construct an answer**. Students are often frustrated if a dialogue does not finish with a conclusion or answer. That is not to say we should always answer a question—there are many times when it is impossible to do so or more beneficial not to do so. Nonetheless, you will find times when it is better to try to construct some sort of consensus.

9. **Dialogue: Final thoughts**. Even if you do come to consensus, it might also be worthwhile to give each student the opportunity to share *his or her* final thoughts with the community. Ask for volunteers or go around the circle, allowing students to say "pass" if they prefer not to speak.

10. **Review**. Invite reflective and evaluative comments about the inquiry. The review sheet in Appendix 1 would be helpful for this, as would the thoughts of some Dialogue Detectives (see Chapter 6) if indeed you've chosen any students to be Dialogue Detectives. Bear in mind, this review can happen during the dialogue as well as at the end. The guiding questions should always be along the lines of "What went well?" and "What could be improved?"

11.6 • P4C SEQUENCE—IN DEPTH

As mentioned earlier, the following sequence is for guidance only. You do not need to follow all the steps. The most important ones are numbers 1, 2, 6, 7 and 8. The others are only if you have time and if you want to give your students the opportunity to create and choose the question for inquiry. Otherwise, you can create the question yourself and give it to your students for them to explore.

1. Prepare

When setting up a P4C dialogue with a group, it is always best to sit in a circle. This indicates that everyone will be thinking *together*—as opposed to listening to one person or viewing a screen.

2. Share a Stimulus

> **Philosophy begins in wonder. If you can find something that has no obvious answer, no particular moral, or something that is baffling in some way, then it should prove to be a good starting point for philosophical inquiry with your students.**

For example:

- Artwork—Almost anything will do, but particularly work by Pablo Picasso, Banksy, Rita Pearce or, a personal favorite of ours for encouraging inquiry with students, Keith Haring (see www.haringkids.com).

- Picture books—Most books have an array of themes that could provoke curiosity. Sure-fire winners include stories by Julia Donaldson, Anthony Browne, David McKee, Edward Monkton or Shaun Tan.

- Video stories—We have created a playlist on YouTube that includes some of our favorite stories to begin a thoughtful discussion with children. Search for Videos for P4C Inquiries on the YouTube channel "jabulani4" or on Vimeo (https://vimeo .com/challenginglearning).

As with all dialogues, P4C works best when participants sit in a circle.

3. Identify Issues and Concepts

One of the best ways to get your students to find the main ideas in a stimulus is to help them identify the key concepts. A concept is a general idea that groups things together according to accepted characteristics.

Here are several important concepts that students would do well to understand:

A key concept should always be at the heart of a P4C dialogue.

Arts: beauty, art, imagination, reproduction, real, copy, meaning

Citizenship: rights, duties, justice, fairness, freedom, welfare, community, enterprise

Design: purpose, economy, value, elegance, simplicity, effectiveness, originality

Humanities/social studies: justice, globalization, nation, interpretation, history, truth, cause

Information, communication technology: knowledge, entertainment, game, reality, legality, morality, social media

Literature: love, democracy, fairness, justice, goodness, power, anger

Religious education: belief, faith, truth, morality, tolerance, customs, rites

Science: science, experiment, evidence, knowledge, theory, fair test, proof, cause, reaction

4. Create Questions

Some of the more famous philosophical questions include the following: What is the meaning of life? Is there a god? Is torture justifiable? If a tree falls but no one hears it, then did it make a sound? However, there are an almost limitless number of philosophical questions, and these can be created from almost any concept.

> Pairing question stems with one or more well-chosen concepts will help students create thought-provoking questions.

▶ Figure 35: Question Stems

Question Stem	Example
What is . . .?	What is love?
What makes . . .?	What makes a friend special?
Would you be . . .?	Would you be the same person if you had a different name?
How do we know what . . .?	How do we know what courage is?
Always or never	Should we always obey the law?
What if . . .?	What if people had never learned how to tell lies?
Is it possible . . .?	Is it possible to be normal and different at the same time?
When . . .?	When is happiness a bad emotion?
Who . . .?	Who decides what art is?
Can we . . .?	Can we ever know someone else—or even ourselves—completely?
Why do we say . . .?	Why do we say "seeing is believing"?
What is the difference between . . .?	What is the difference between being a friend and being friendly?

In Figure 35 you can see some of the most useful question stems. We have put them together as a card so that you can photocopy it and give it to your students (or download a higher-res version from www.challenginglearning.com).

If your students select a concept and then put it together with one of these question stems, they are likely to create a thought-provoking, philosophical question worth investigating.

All of the question stems shown in Figure 35 are productive. The last one is our favorite, though, because it works so well in many different contexts. It is also a question stem that you can throw into a dialogue when things are going a bit slow. The effect is almost always a positive one.

Some examples of the "What is the difference between . . ." questions that you might like to have up your sleeve, either as lesson starters or as dialogue developers, are shown in Figure 36. Again, we have made them into a card for easy printing and keeping by your side when running a dialogue with your students.

► Figure 36: **What Is the Difference Between . . .**

What is the difference between . . .

- Love and Hate?
- Stories and Lies?
- Thinking and Believing?
- Names and Nicknames?
- Happiness and Contentment?
- The Five Senses and the Sixth Sense?
- Sports and War?
- Watching and Dreaming?
- Reality and Virtual Reality?
- Trying and Achieving?
- Art and Entrepreneurship?

- Children and Adults?
- Wisdom and Experience?
- Knowledge and Evidence?
- Fame and Infamy?
- Rights and Responsibilities?
- Collaboration and Individuality?
- Inspiration and Dedication?
- Good and Bad?
- Democracy and Dictatorship?
- Faith and Trust?
- Power and Aggression?

> Asking what the difference is between two or more concepts can lead to excellent exploratory dialogue.

5. Choose and Air Questions

When using P4C to create dialogue with your students, collect one open-ended question from each group. If one of the groups has more than one question, then ask them to select what they think is their best one. Altogether, from all the small groups combined, try to collect no more than seven questions. If necessary, arrange the size of each small group so that you have a maximum of seven groups in the class.

After collecting one question from each group, give your students time to air the questions; this could be done by getting authors to give a brief insight into their own question or by asking for volunteers to say why they think each question in turn is a particularly good one.

> Once students have created philosophical questions, they should air them before voting to identify the best one.

Once the questions have been aired, it is time to take a vote. In the first few sessions with your students, it is probably enough to encourage them to pick their favorite question. After a while, though, you should be encouraging them to select the best one. To do this, you will need to agree on some criteria for what constitutes the best, for example, the most open and philosophical one, the most problematic or thought-provoking one or the one most likely to create a range of opinions and disagreements.

Here are some other examples:

- questions that offer the widest selection of possible answers
- questions that deal with concepts most central to students' lives
- questions that raise the most contestable concepts
- questions that provide the greatest chance of differing viewpoints
- questions that can't be answered with a simple yes or no

It may not be obvious which is the best question, and in some regards it may be impossible to decide for sure. However, the very process of selecting criteria and using these to make a decision can be a worthwhile end in itself.

Then, when it comes to the voting, there are many ways to go. Following are some popular ones.

Single vote: Each person gets one vote. The question that attracts the most votes is chosen for further discussion.

Omni-vote: Each person can vote as many times as desired. (Although it is worth reminding younger children that if they all vote for all the questions, there won't be one that stands out!) The omni-vote is generally the best method of voting for groups new to P4C.

Multi-vote: Each person gets a set number of votes—say, three—that can then be spread between three questions or placed into one or two questions.

Single transferable vote: This works well if you lay out the questions on the floor and ask students to each stand next to one of the questions. You can then ask the students standing next to the questions with fewest votes to recast their vote onto one of the front-runners.

6. Dialogue: First Thoughts

This stage is all about encouraging your students to share their first responses to the chosen question.

Give all your students some reflection time before inviting first thoughts from a few volunteers. Resist the temptation to question or challenge too soon. Encourage all the other students to listen attentively and with respect.

Do *not* feel compelled to get every student to speak!

There is a commonly held belief that we should try to ensure all students say at least one thing in each discussion. This is nonsensical because there are some people who do their very best thinking when saying *nothing* (while others find it easier to think well by saying lots).

One justification for this can be found in the work of Katharine Cook Briggs and her daughter, Isabel Briggs Myers. During World War II, they created the Myers-Briggs Type Indicator (MBTI) to help women identify the sort of wartime jobs in which they would be most comfortable and effective. Their work was based on the theories of Carl Jung.

Of the four pairs of preferences proposed in the MBTI assessment tool, one set of opposites focused on the difference between extraversion and introversion. It identified that some people tend to act–reflect–act (extraversion), whereas others reflect–act–reflect (introversion). Or put another way:

Introverted thinking is about *thinking to talk.*

Extraverted thinking is about *talking to think.*

Of course, the MBTI is a personality test and should therefore be taken with a very big pinch of salt. It is also context-related: how many of us are introverted when dragged to a party of complete strangers but extroverted when playing host at our own party? Context obviously matters! So it is simply not true to say that we are either one way or the other *all the time.*

The key is that some people—students included—*typically* find it easier to think if they don't have to say anything, whereas others *typically* find talking lots helps to clarify their thinking. Contrast this with many school-based discussions in which the teacher begins by saying:

"I'm going to pass this fluffy owl around the circle. When you've got it then, and only then, is it your turn to talk!"

Imagine if you're in the mood for some introverted thinking and you've been given the fluffy owl first. What do you do? Everyone is looking at you expectantly, but you haven't had time to think what you might say. As the pressure builds, your teacher reminds you to say "pass" if you want to. The problem is you know if you *do* say "pass," then everyone will think you're a dimwit. Meanwhile, around the other side of the circle, there's an extraverted thinker desperate to say something, with words and ideas ready to pour out of every orifice! Eventually, the extraverted child shouts out, and the teacher barks at them for breaking the rules.

Oh, the joys of teaching (and yes, so very many times, we were *that* teacher).

Better ways to run dialogues that encourage thinking in both an extraverted *and* introverted manner include the following:

Reflection time—Give everyone a moment to either collect their own thoughts or share their first ideas (very quietly) with the person next to them (see Section 7.1).

Pause—Pause the P4C session halfway through to give some thinking time, either overnight or for a short period during the school day. A good time to pause is once the voting has been completed (see Choose and Air Questions above) so that your students can reflect on the question that has been chosen.

Inner circle and outer circle—This works particularly well if you have a group of twenty or more. Split the group in two and get half the students to sit in a circle, with the other half sat around the outside of the circle. The outer group can record the dialogue—with a mind map, concept map or similar—and jot down their own thoughts. If you then swap the groups around periodically—perhaps every 10 minutes or so—then everyone will have a chance to reflect quietly *and* speak if they want to. This idea is covered in more depth in Chapter 6.

> Varying the ways of engaging students will keep introverted and extraverted thinkers more engaged.

Of course, many teachers might still worry if some students don't speak. However, we don't know that students are concentrating even if they *do* speak! Many students have learned phrases and tactics designed to give the impression that they are focused when actually their mind is elsewhere.

So whether you are in discussion with one student or a whole group of students, we recommend the following:

a. Pause and reflect time.

b. Feasibility language: Phrases such as *perhaps, maybe* or *I was wondering* promote a sense of open-mindedness and exploration, which is something that's vital for inquiry.

c. Thinking: Remind students that the most important thing is to *think* about the question. So long as everyone does that, it is up to individuals whether or not to share their views with others.

7. Dialogue: Build and Challenge

Once students have shared their first thoughts, begin building on and/or challenging the ideas they've expressed. Chapter 3 goes into more detail about ways to do this. For now, though, following are a few ideas.

> Once students have aired their initial thoughts, the P4C facilitator should encourage everyone to build on and challenge others' ideas.

RPC (Repeat–Paraphrase–Connect)—When a student has expressed his or her first idea, get others to *repeat* word for word what's been said, *paraphrase* by saying the same thing in a different way or *connect* what was said to an idea of their own.

Meaning—A particularly effective strategy is to respond to a student's contribution by asking if anybody else knows what the student meant. Some students will feel certain that they understood, so ask them to explain. If there's just two of you in the discussion, then you could try explaining what you think the other person meant. Either way, make sure you then ask the first person if indeed that was what they meant. Usually, the explanation is close to the intended meaning but not exactly so, which gives the first person an opportunity to clarify even more. This strategy also teaches us there is often a marked difference between what someone says and how others understand it.

Agree—A simple (and effective) convention is to ask everyone taking part in a dialogue to begin their first few responses with "I agree with . . . because . . ." as this requires participants to listen carefully to what has been said before.

Questions That Build

> Here are some questions that help build on others' ideas.

There are many questions that invite students to express themselves further and to build on what has already been said. Here are a few examples:

- Can we think of an example of that?
- What are the strengths of that idea?
- Why do you say that?
- Are there any other reasons you can think of?
- What evidence is there to support what you are saying?

Ways to Challenge

> Here are some questions that help to challenge others' ideas.

a. **Disagree**—As with the "I agree" convention, this is a simple and effective approach that aids thinking. This time everyone should begin their responses with "I disagree with . . . because . . ."

b. **Create cognitive conflict**—Setting up a conflict of opinions in an individual's mind causes that person to reflect more urgently on what it is he or she actually thinks. This in turn leads to greater engagement and a more energetic search for a resolution. We go into this strategy in depth in another book in this series, *Challenging Learning Through Questioning* (Nottingham & Renton, in press).

One of the easiest ways to set up cognitive conflict is to use:

If A = B, then does B = A?

For instance, if you ask what a holiday (A) is and a student responds, "Not being at school" (this is B), you can then ask, "Does this mean that if I'm not at school, then I'm on holiday?" (For example, every evening and weekend? Or if I'm too ill to go to school?)

For more examples of this approach, see pages 59–75 of *Challenging Learning* (Nottingham, 2016).

c. **Critical thinking**—The word *critical* comes from the Greek *kriticos* meaning "able to make judgments." This is a useful reminder when running P4C sessions:

are your students expressing received ideas or are they weighing up pros and cons and making a reasoned judgment? If it is the latter, then they are probably engaging in critical thinking. If it is the former, then no matter how articulate they might be, they may still be engaging only in opinionated debate.

Below are some steps for developing critical thinking. There are many more, including the application of formal and informal logic as well as judgment making, but the following are good starting points.

a. Ask for reasons to support the opinions already expressed. For example, if one of your students has said, "I think it is wrong to lie," then ask for a reason (e.g., because then people won't trust you).

b. Develop a critical thinking argument. This is a claim that is intended to be persuasive, has a conclusion and is supported by at least one reason.

c. Examine the quality of each claim in terms of credibility, assumptions it might be based on, response to counter-claims and so on.

Questions That Challenge

There are many questions that invite students to examine what they, and others, have said. Here are a few examples:

- What alternative ways of looking at this are there?

- How can we verify or disprove that assumption?

- What would happen if the opposite were true?

- What are the weaknesses of that idea?

- What are the consequences of that assumption?

8. Dialogue: Construct an Answer

Even if a question is patently open-ended and philosophical, with no agreed answer, students can still feel frustrated if they do not arrive at *an* answer. In school, and often at home, we tend to lead students to believe that learning is about finding the right answer to every question. Yet there are many questions that do not have one agreed-on right answer, for example, "What is the best work-life balance?" "What can we do about climate change?" "What is the right thing to say to someone who is grieving?" "Why do seemingly good people commit atrocities?"

To help students gradually learn that many questions do not have one right answer, we advocate leaving at least some philosophical questions unanswered, even after a long and fruitful inquiry. This will also help students learn how to manage uncertainty.

That said, it might be more constructive, particularly in the early stages of your students' philosophical development, to help them come to *some* sort of resolution. It is likely that the process of inquiry will have generated a myriad of possibilities. To help students sort through these, you could help them make links using one of the following approaches:

Ranking—Have students choose the best of the bunch. For example, if they have been thinking about friendship, your students will probably have considered such qualities as trust, familiarity, enjoying each other's company, wanting to spend time with each other, knowing the bad as well as the good about each other, having a shared history and so on. So you could now ask them to rank these qualities from most important to least important or most common to least common. Alternatively,

> Ways to develop critical thinking include asking for reasons, examining claims and checking assumptions.

> Constructing an answer by listing, ranking or categorizing solutions can offer closure to those students who are irritated by questions that seem to have no answer.

you could ask them to select the three qualities that they believe are necessary for every friendship.

Relationships—Describing the underlying concept of the question *in relation to another concept* often helps students shape their ideas more satisfactorily, for example, identifying what a friend is in relation to a best friend, what courage is in relation to foolhardiness, what reality is in relation to make-believe and so on.

Categorize—Using tools such as Venn diagrams (see Section 9.7) or inference squares (Nottingham, 2013, p. 121) can help students distinguish between two (or more) interrelated concepts. For example, you can use a Venn diagram to draw distinctions between help and advice or between telling lies and being wrong. And you can use an inference square to separate what we know for certain from what we think we know or would like to know. These strategies can bring clarity to students' thinking.

9. Dialogue: Final Thoughts

> If time allows, then a good way to end a P4C dialogue is with "final words."

It is often a good idea to give students a sense of closure by opting for one of these approaches:

Last words—Give every student a final opportunity to respond to the question or to something heard during the inquiry. If you have been thinking together with a large group, it might be appropriate to offer the opportunity only to those who haven't spoken or to allow some students to pass.

Voting—Round off the question by taking a vote. Ensure there are three options: "yes," "no" and "not sure." Including the "not sure" option emphasizes that most philosophical questions are not black or white but tend to be shades of gray.

Final five—Restrict the number of words each participant can use in the final words to five. Not only does this prevent some students waffling on for ages, but it also tends to focus the minds of everyone involved, encouraging them to select only the most pertinent or significant words.

> **A phrase that captures the spirit of P4C is "Not all of our questions answered, but all of our answers questioned." So asking all participants to verbalize the questions they still have about the topic would capture the inquiring spirit nicely.**

10. Dialogue Review

Invite reflective and evaluative comments about the inquiry. The review sheet in Appendix 1 would be helpful for this, as would the thoughts of some Dialogue Detectives (see Chapter 6) if indeed you've used this strategy. Bear in mind, this review can happen during the dialogue as well as at the end. The guiding questions should always be along the lines of "What went well?" and "What could be improved?"

This chapter has shown you how to begin using Philosophy for Children. The key points have included the following:

1. The aim of P4C is to emphasize many of the values of philosophy—wisdom, reflection, reasoning and reasonableness—and to ensure that they are part of every student's education.

2. A central concept of P4C is that of the community of inquiry. This can be defined as a reflective approach to classroom dialogue built up over time with a single group of students. The community embodies cooperation, care, respect and safety; the inquiry reaches for understanding, meaning, truth and values supported by reasons.

3. A question to start a philosophical dialogue will contain, or at least imply, a concept from life and learning that is both important and questionable. It will also be an open question in the sense that it will not be asked from a position of authority with a preconceived answer in mind.

4. P4C begins in wonder. If you can find something that has no obvious answer, no particular moral, or something that is baffling in some way, then it is likely to be a good starting point for philosophical inquiry with your students.

5. P4C is not about listening and talking; it is about listening and *thinking*. Some students do their best thinking by saying nothing, whereas others do their best thinking out loud. A community of inquiry should support both of these approaches to thinking.

6. Feasibility language (phrases such as *perhaps, maybe* or *I was wondering*) will promote the sense of open-mindedness and exploration that should be at the heart of any dialogue, including P4C dialogue.

7. The key parts of P4C that help build dialogue brilliantly include first thoughts, build and challenge, constructing an answer, and final words.

11.8 • NEXT STEPS AND FURTHER READING

Here are some suggestions for what you could do next so that you get the most out of this chapter:

1. Try out a few P4C episodes with your students to see how they respond to it.

2. As a variation to the typical P4C sequence shown in this chapter, try the Dialogue Detectives (Chapter 6) and the Panel Dialogue (Section 5.4 B) strategies described in earlier chapters.

3. Write a list of philosophical concepts that you think arise in a subject area you teach. Choose five of those questions and present them to students. Ask your students to choose the one they would most like to discuss and say why. Then take a vote and discuss the one chosen using strategies 6 to 9 in this chapter.

4. Use Think-Pair-Share (see Section 7.1) as part of your P4C sessions. It will help students rehearse their ideas and will give them more confidence to share their ideas with others.

5. During your P4C sessions, use the restatement and reformulation strategies (Sections 3.4 and 3.5) during P4C steps 7, 8 and 9.

6. Use the language of reasoning (see Figure 3 in Section 4.1) during your P4C sessions. It will help students develop more complex answers to their questions.

7. Add the strategies from this section to your Repertoire and Judgment Notes at the back of this book.

8. Take a look at some of the many excellent resources available on www.p4c.com.

We recommend reading the following books and websites to find out more about P4C:

Cam, P. (1998). *Thinking together.* Alexandria, NSW, Australia: Hale & Iremonger.

Hymer, B., & Sutcliffe, R. (2012). *P4C pocketbook.* Alresford, UK: Teachers' Pocketbooks.

Law, S., & Postgate, D. (2011). *The complete philosophy files.* London, UK: Orion Children's Books.

Stanley, S. (2012). *Why think? Philosophical play from 3–11.* London, UK: Continuum.

ICPIC, an international council for P4C: www.icpic.org

International P4C Cooperative: www.p4c.com

Sapere, a UK-based charity supporting P4C: www.sapere.org.uk

> "Over the last week or so we've been asking you for ideas about what subjects ought to be taught in schools but are not taught. Now, there have been many suggestions . . . but the overwhelming winner—you may be surprised by this—was philosophy."
>
> (Humphrys, 2004)

DIALOGUE EXERCISES IN P4C

12.0 • PREVIEW

This chapter explains how using exercises can enhance the way in which Philosophy for Children develops dialogue. These exercises will stimulate ongoing dialogue around important questions and concepts.

Two types of exercise are explored in this chapter:

- make a choice, give a reason
- concept stretching

> Rather like drills in sports, dialogue exercises give participants an opportunity to practice individual skills in isolation before putting them back into context.

12.1 • DIALOGUE EXERCISES

Exercises are integral to Philosophy for Children (P4C) and to the process of dialogue and inquiry. Exercises will (a) help to practice a skill, (b) have a specific purpose and (c) use a thinking process.

There are at least three purposes for exercises in P4C; in any given exercise the purposes may overlap:

- to establish the language of reasoning using terms such as *assumption* appropriately

- to establish habits such as giving and asking for reasons and adjusting one's opinion in the light of discussion

- to explore a concept or argument in a more focused way than is possible in open discussion.

Below are some examples of exercises together with explanations about why and how they might be used.

When you start P4C, try out some exercises early on. You can introduce them as stand-alone activities or connect them to your ongoing inquiries, structured by the stages of inquiry. Many of the dialogue structures (see Chapter 6) can be used as organizing structures for exercises. For example, Corners can be used for "Make a Choice, Give a Reason"; Opinion Lines can be used for "Concept Stretching: Fairness."

12.2 • MAKE A CHOICE, GIVE A REASON

Make a Choice, Give a Reason is an excellent drill for identifying reasons, assumptions, similarities and consequences.

This is one way to help your students practice terms such as *reason, assumption, similar* and *consequence*. It also helps to establish habits of agreeing, disagreeing, changing opinions and careful listening.

What to do: Give your students a choice. Ask them to indicate their choice by gesture (such as thumbs up for "yes," thumbs down for "no") or by movement to different areas of the classroom. Ask them to share their reasons for their choice. After sufficient reasons have been aired, ask which ones were similar and which different. Ask if any students have changed their minds or qualified their opinions in any way.

Examples: Start with examples that are fun and easy to agree or disagree with. Later, include items that matter more to you and your students. Here are some items that you could offer:

- Which are the best: dogs or cats? (This question is just to get the activity going in an enjoyable way so students can feel comfortable with the process. It could also lead into some practice with language of reasoning moves like asking for criteria or identifying assumptions.)

- If you could choose between being invisible and having everlasting life, which would you choose?

- If you could choose between being invisible, having everlasting life or having the gift of making the best decisions in life, which would you choose?

- If you could choose between a fair teacher, a kind teacher or a strict teacher, which would you choose?

After your students have exchanged reasons, it is easy to see where terms like *assumption* or *criteria* might be introduced as a next step.

For example, in considering a choice between invisibility and everlasting life, your students might assume that people with everlasting life would not age physically and mentally but get stuck at the age they liked best. Questioning this assumption could lead to some imaginative thinking.

In the "choice of teacher" question, some might say they would prefer a good teacher. Then you could ask what qualities make a teacher "good." These moves enable us to share the hidden thinking that lies behind judgments. This prepares your students to make more complete arguments later.

12.3 • CONCEPT STRETCHING: FAIRNESS

(James) *Concept Stretching* is a term my colleagues at www.p4c.com and I created to describe a process of exploring and stretching the limits of understanding of concepts. Here is an example based on the concept of fairness.

Fairness has a number of dimensions. Depending on the context, it can mean the following:

1. Just deserts. Getting what you deserve. Being rewarded on merit.

2. Equality. Being treated the same as others. Having equal opportunities. Perhaps having equal outcomes in some situations.

3. Being treated appropriately. Having your needs met or at least recognized.

What makes fairness an interesting concept to explore with your students is that they will probably find it quite difficult to agree on what people *really* deserve and to what extent privilege or disadvantage should be recognized. For example, should all children get the same rewards from their teachers? Should all parents be told how much they are allowed to spend on their children so that all children are the same?

In the exercise below, invite your students to give reasons for why they think the example is fair or unfair. Remember, it is important to explore the principles behind the reasons. Introducing words like *equal, same* and *deserve* will help if students are having difficulty.

When the principles come to light, there will still be work to do in expanding the short context with some "If . . . then" reasoning. For example, in considering point 2 below, one of your students might say, "If I have to tidy up another person's mess then it isn't fair." You might follow this up by asking for counter-examples: "Would it *ever* be fair to be asked to tidy up another person's mess?"

How fair is each of these scenarios?

1. A student has difficulty reading. The teacher spends more time with that student than with the other students. Sometimes other students have to wait for help.

2. A teacher makes all students tidy up at the end of the day.

3. A student is badly behaved. The teacher speaks harshly to that student but speaks in a friendly way to other students who behave well.

4. A teacher decides to give all students an award for something, even if that means some get awards for things other students are better at.

Activity for Five- to Eight-Year-Olds

Pick two children. Give one of them one sweet and the other two sweets, and ask if that's okay. Swap them around, such that the first child now has two sweets and the other one has one. Is that fair? Now take the sweets away from both of them and give them to other children. Ask whether it's fair now.

Also ask, "Is it fair that I should be able to give my sweets to whoever I want to? Is it fair to take something away from someone, once it has been given? Why or why not?"

Questions to follow up with:

- Does fair mean being the same as someone?

- Or does it mean everyone having the same things?

> Concept Stretching is one way to explore the boundaries and nuances of meanings.

> Here are some examples of Concept Stretchers for young students.

- How do you know if something's fair or not?
- Why should people try to be fair?
- What is unfair?
- If Lucy pinches Amy, is it fair for Amy to pinch Lucy?

Activity for Eight- to Twelve-Year-Olds

Ask your students to help you set up an imaginary running race, and change the variables that make up the teams, asking each time whether the race would be fair.

For example, draw attention to the following:

- Different length legs
- Newest trainers versus oldest trainers
- Boys versus girls
- Oldest versus youngest
- What would be the fairest way to set up the teams? Give reasons.
- Would a draw be the fairest possible result? Give reasons.
- Could handicapping the best runners (for example, by giving them heavy rucksacks, staggered starts or obstacles) make the race fairer, or would that be unfair to the best runners? Give reasons.
- If a runner is unlucky to get knocked over by accident, is that unfair?
- If a team wins the race by cheating, is that unfair? Why?

Activity for Teenagers

Would it be fair to share out all the food in the world equally? If so, would it be fair for me to take food from your house and send it to children who have very little food?

- Would it be fair for everyone to earn the same wage?
- Is it fair to have rich people and poor people?
- Is fairness possible within a family?
- Is fairness possible within school?
- Is it fair when bad things happen to good people?
- Is it fair when good things happen to bad people?
- Would it be fair for someone who's desperate to jump to the front of the toilet queue?
- Is it fair to always go with what the majority want?
- Is it fair to put on school trips that not everyone can afford to go on?
- Is it fair that eighteen-year-olds have a lower minimum wage than twenty-one-year-olds?
- Would it be fair to torture the torturer, terrorize the terrorist or murder the murderer?
- Is fairness possible (or even desirable) in society?
- How could fairness be achieved?

Here are some examples of Concept Stretchers for pre-teens.

Here are some examples of Concept Stretchers for teenagers.

- Is survival of the fittest fair?

- Is it possible to construct a fair test in science?

In Figure 37 you will find a set of examples for your students to think about. You can print this sheet out and give it to pairs or small groups to complete.

▶ Figure 37: Fair or Unfair

Are these examples fair or unfair?		Fair	Unfair	?	Reason	
1	Everyone in the school is given the same amount of homework.					
2	Doctors are paid more than teachers.					
3	Men are paid more than women for doing the same job.					
4	Everyone is given a prize on Sports Day.					
5	Children in some countries can't afford to go to school.					
6	Some people live in very big houses.					
7	A starving woman steals a loaf of bread to feed her family.					
8	A student steals a CD from a shop.					
9	Children are not allowed to drive cars.					
10	Disabled people are allowed to park for free.					
11	Someone breaks the law so is sent to prison.					
12	A grandmother can't pay her property tax so is sent to prison.					

12.4 • REVIEW

This chapter has shown you two types of exercises you can use to develop dialogue through the P4C approach. The key points have included the following:

1. Exercises help your students practice terms such as *reason, assumption, similar* and *consequence.*

2. Exercises develop habits such as giving and asking for reasons and adjusting opinions in the light of discussion.

3. Concept Stretching is the process of exploring and stretching the limits of understanding of concepts.

12.5 • NEXT STEPS AND FURTHER READING

Here are some suggestions for what you could do next so that you get the most out of this chapter:

1. Try out both types of exercise with your students.

2. Create an exercise of your own based on either of the two types of exercise shared in this chapter.

3. There are a lot of examples of Concept Stretchers (in English) for members of www.p4c.com, so that would be worth checking out.

4. Add the strategies from this section to your Repertoire and Judgment Notes at the back of this book.

Both of these books have a lot of P4C exercises in them:

Nottingham, J. (2013). *Encouraging learning*. Abingdon, UK: Routledge.

Nottingham, J. (2016). *Challenging learning* (2nd ed.). Abingdon, UK: Routledge.

Here are a couple of useful websites:

www.p4c.com (subscription resources and collaboration site)

www.thephilosophyman.com (authored by Jason Buckley)

APPENDIX 1: DIALOGUE DETECTIVES
(Relates to Chapter 6)

A. The Spirit of Dialogue (Listening and Responding)

Scale: 0 = hardly ever   1 = some/sometimes   2 = most/most of the time   3 = almost all the time

1.	Did people encourage each other to speak (e.g., encouraging gestures, taking turns)?	(altruism)	0	1	2	3
2.	Did people focus their attention on the speaker?	(attentiveness)	0	1	2	3
3.	Did people avoid interrupting or rushing the speaker?	(patience)	0	1	2	3
4.	Did people stick to their own convictions?	(courage)	0	1	2	3
5.	Did people keep their contributions brief?	(concision)	0	1	2	3
6.	Did people stick to the question?	(tenacity and discipline)	0	1	2	3
7.	Did people show a willingness to change their minds?	(openness)	0	1	2	3
8.	Did people listen carefully to ideas different from their own?	(tolerance)	0	1	2	3
9.	Did people recall others' ideas and put their names to them?	(respect)	0	1	2	3
10.	Did people try to build on others' ideas?	(constructiveness)	0	1	2	3

B. The Practice of Thinking Together (Questioning and Reasoning)

Scale: 0 = not observed   1 = observed at least once   2 = observed now and then   3 = observed often

11.	Did people ask open and inviting questions?	(curiosity)	0	1	2	3
12.	Did people ask for clarification/definition of meaning?	(precision)	0	1	2	3
13.	Did people question assumptions or conclusions?	(skepticism)	0	1	2	3
14.	Did people ask for examples or evidence?	(doubt)	0	1	2	3
15.	Did people ask for reasons or criteria?	(rationality)	0	1	2	3
16.	Did people give examples or counter-examples?	(realism)	0	1	2	3
17.	Did people give reasons or justifications?	(reasonableness)	0	1	2	3
18.	Did people offer or explore alternative viewpoints?	(creativity)	0	1	2	3
19.	Did people make connections or analogies?	(connectivity)	0	1	2	3
20.	Did people make distinctions?	(perceptiveness)	0	1	2	3

APPENDIX 2: LOUIS PASTEUR SCRIPT
(Relates to Section 8.9.2)

Research Groups

Louis Pasteur

Cast of six readers

Inquirers

Reader 1: John

Reader 2: Kerrie

Reader 3: Laura

Reader 4: Daniel

Scientists

Reader 5: Louis Pasteur

Reader 6: Max Von Pettenkofer

If the script is performed for an audience, then I suggest the two scientists sit together in the center on revolving stools. They have their backs to the audience until their first lines in the script, when they should turn around. After their last lines in the script they turn their backs to the audience again. The inquirers should sit on stools or chairs—one pair either side of the scientists, slightly sloping upstage. I suggest John and Kerrie as one pair, Laura and Daniel as the other.

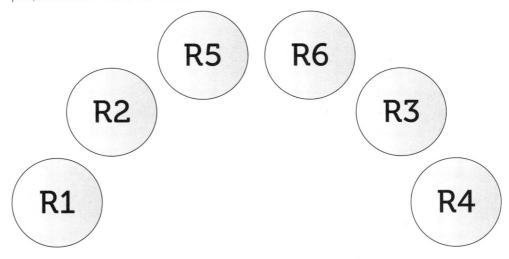

Part One: Pasteur's Discovery

LAURA	Our study topic this week is Louis Pasteur.
DANIEL	Who was he?
LAURA	Why is he important?
KERRIE	What's his story?
JOHN	Let's read through what we've written so far.
DANIEL	Louis Pasteur was a scientist who lived in France more than a hundred years ago. At that time, a disease called anthrax was killing a lot of farm animals.
LAURA	Deaths of sheep from anthrax were costing French farmers $140,000 a year. Farmers feared they would catch the disease too. Some humans had died from anthrax.
JOHN	It was caused by bacteria. They multiplied very quickly if they got into the bloodstream through a cut or a scratch. A few hours after the disease took hold, millions of bacteria turned the blood black. Arteries and veins got blocked. Death followed soon after.
KERRIE	At that time, Pasteur was studying another disease called chicken cholera. He was injecting hens with different vaccines and then injecting them with cholera bacteria. None of his vaccines worked. All the hens died.
DANIEL	One day some of his cholera bacteria were left in the open air. When he injected hens with these, they didn't die. Pasteur must have thought:
JOHN	(*Role-playing Pasteur*) Leaving the cholera bacteria in the open must have weakened them in some way. The strange thing is that when I injected the same hens again with strong cholera, they survived. I wonder . . . does a weakened dose of a disease work as a vaccine against a stronger one? No hens have survived a strong dose before. This is the first time it has happened. There must be a reason.
LAURA	He set to work on finding a vaccine for anthrax by leaving anthrax germs in the open air to weaken them.
KERRIE	On May 5, 1881, a famous experiment took place to prove or disprove Pasteur's theory. A huge crowd came to watch.
JOHN	(*Role-playing Pasteur and standing*) Ladies and gentlemen, I have been given sixty sheep. I have vaccinated twenty-five sheep with my weakened dose of anthrax. I will re-vaccinate them twelve days from now. Two weeks after that, they will be injected with a strong dose of anthrax. Another twenty-five unvaccinated sheep will also be given a strong dose of anthrax. Ten sheep will be left alone. I predict that the vaccinated sheep will still be alive thirty days from now.

LAURA	The crowd came back on June 2. Pasteur was proved right. Every one of the unvaccinated sheep was dead or dying. Every one of the vaccinated sheep was alive and well. So were the untouched animals.
DANIEL	Pasteur was a hero. That day marked the beginning of the end for many infectious diseases that had killed so many people in the past. That's what it says in the textbook, anyway.

Part Two: Theories and Experiments

JOHN	I have a question. How could Pasteur know for sure that he'd found the right vaccine after trying it on only twenty-five sheep?
LAURA	What do you mean, John?
JOHN	Well, imagine if a big bin suddenly appeared on the school field. Because I'm brave I get to the bin first. I reach into the bin and pick out twenty-five things. They are all chocolate bars.
DANIEL	Is this a dream you have every night or something?
JOHN	Daniel, listen! The first twenty-five things are chocolate bars. How do I know the twenty-sixth thing won't be something else— even a bomb? How did Pasteur know that twenty-five sheep would be enough to test his vaccine?
LAURA	But this is different. No sheep had ever survived anthrax before, and there must have been thousands of deaths. The vaccinated sheep all survived.
DANIEL	Laura is right. And on top of that, every one of the other sheep who'd been injected with anthrax germs died. There's not much chance of that happening for no reason.
KERRIE	It fit in with Pasteur's theory too. He could explain why it happened that way.
PASTEUR	You ask an interesting question, John. Were twenty-five sheep enough to prove my theory? Make up your own minds. Imagine what it was like trying to persuade a farmer that I could stop his sheep getting anthrax by injecting them with anthrax. I was lucky to get any sheep to work on. But I was famous, and that always helps. I'm Louis Pasteur, by the way.

Part Three: A Debate About the Causes of Anthrax

LAURA	Are you a ghost?
PASTEUR	Let's just say a voice from the past.
VON PETTENKOFER	Can I say something, Louis?
KERRIE	And who are you?

VON PETTENKOFER   Max Von Pettenkofer, a German scientist. I lived at the same time as Louis Pasteur.

PASTEUR   Max didn't believe that bacteria caused disease. He even drank a glass of water full of cholera bacteria to show his faith.

VON PETTENKOFER   And I survived. Doesn't that prove something?

PASTEUR   It proves you were very lucky. Haven't you kept in touch with the world since you died, Max? Scientists agree that bacteria and other kinds of germs do cause diseases. Vaccines can help to stop diseases spreading.

VON PETTENKOFER   I was wrong in some ways, but in some ways I was right. It depends what we mean by that word *cause*. Why don't you tell them about the worms, Louis, and why one field was deadly to sheep but another was harmless.

PASTEUR   What are you getting at, Max?

VON PETTENKOFER   Let's hear the story. Then I'll explain.

PASTEUR   One day I was walking in a field of sheep. I noticed that the ground in one part of the field was a different color from the rest. As I got closer, I noticed lots of worm casts—the soil worms push out as they tunnel along. I asked the farmer about this, and he told me a few of his sheep had died of anthrax. He buried them in the field. I guessed that the worms had been feeding off the dead sheep. They brought the anthrax bacteria to the surface, and the live sheep ate grass with the bacteria on it. But the anthrax could have been passed on in other ways. Sheep with cuts and scratches sometimes rubbed against other sheep with the disease.

VON PETTENKOFER   So was anthrax caused by the bacteria or by the farmer burying the dead sheep in the field or both? And did the farmer keep his sheep healthy enough? What do your young friends think about that?

JOHN   A cause always comes just before the thing it causes. The bacteria getting into the sheep was the last thing to happen before they got ill, so I think the bacteria is the cause.

KERRIE   But if the farmer hadn't buried the dead sheep with anthrax in the same field, the anthrax might not have spread. That set off the chain of events that got the anthrax into all the live sheep.

LAURA   Maybe there are more causes than one. These could both be causes in different ways.

DANIEL   Grass might be the cause. It wouldn't have happened without grass.

KERRIE   Daniel, what do you mean?

DANIEL   If there wasn't grass, Kerrie, the sheep wouldn't have eaten it—so no deadly bacteria.

KERRIE	They would just have died of starvation.
LAURA	Anyway, all sheep eat grass, but not all sheep get anthrax. I think a cause must be something that doesn't happen all the time.
PASTEUR	We could go on saying it couldn't have happened except for this or that, but the thing is it did. We needed a quick way to stop the disease spreading. Our methods worked. They've worked for many other diseases too.
VON PETTENKOFER	You'll never get rid of all the germs in the world, Louis. And even you have to admit that some vaccines don't work very well. There are other ways to stop germs spreading—by taking better care of ourselves and our animals. When people are able to keep clean and well fed, we see less disease; when they aren't, we see more. We also know that healthy people and healthy animals can survive serious diseases—like I survived my drink of cholera. So in a way I was proved right.
PASTEUR	I agree, Max, but we still need vaccines for times when things go wrong and for people who are not strong and healthy.
VON PETTENKOFER	Maybe you are right. But at least our young friends have plenty to think about. Good-bye, Louis.
PASTEUR	Good-bye, Max. You know, Max and I had one thing in common. We always asked questions, and asking good questions is the way to make discoveries. That will never change.

Part Four: Experiments on Animals

KERRIE	I'd like to ask Mr. Pasteur a different kind of question.
PASTEUR	What is that?
KERRIE	(*To Pasteur*) Wasn't it wrong for you to inject all those poor sheep with that terrible disease?
JOHN	No way!
KERRIE	I was asking Mr. Pasteur.
PASTEUR	I'd like to hear what you think . . . what you all think.
JOHN	His discovery saved a lot of lives.
KERRIE	Yes. By killing lots of sheep!
JOHN	Pasteur saved lives. He even saved sheeps' lives. Saving the lives of animals is a good thing, isn't it? What about the thousands of sheep that were dying of anthrax? Only the vaccinated sheep survived in his experiment. Remember?
KERRIE	But so did the ones he left alone. The ones that died only died because he injected them with germs. That's just wrong.

Part Five: Animals, Pests and Property

PASTEUR	Before you go on, I'd better tell you about the Australian rabbits.
JOHN	What rabbits?
PASTEUR	Listen, and then see what you think about me saving animals' lives. Europeans started to make homes in Australia over a hundred years ago. There were no rabbits in Australia at the time, but one man brought them to his farm from Europe. Rabbits liked Australia, but Australia didn't like the rabbits. You see, rabbits have lots of babies very often. In twenty years, there were millions of rabbits. They ate farmers' crops and the grass meant for cows and sheep.
LAURA	What did the farmers do?
PASTEUR	I was invited to go to Australia and kill all the rabbits using the chicken cholera bacteria I had been working with.
KERRIE	What? That's horrible.
PASTEUR	Well, that's part of what I want to say. Farmers owned animals like any other property, and they protected their property. To do that they sometimes had to kill other animals. It might seem horrible to you now, Laura, but it wasn't thought so then. The way we think about what things are right and wrong can change with the times.
KERRIE	I think that is wrong and has always been wrong.
LAURA	What happened? Did all the rabbits die?
PASTEUR	No. In the end, the Australians didn't believe the chicken cholera would work. I returned to France. The problem with rabbits got worse, and in 1950 another disease, myxomatosis, was used to kill millions of them.
KERRIE	So they were murdered.
PASTEUR	Murder is a strong word, Kerrie. You will have to decide for yourselves if it fits. I worked on saving sheep in France and killing rabbits in Australia. I did the best job I could, and I thought both jobs helped people. It's up to people at the time to decide what they think animals are for and how they should be treated. It's up to you. Good-bye—and keep asking questions.
KERRIE	I know what I think.
JOHN	Hang on, Kerrie. Last year there was an ants' nest under our house. Every morning our kitchen was crawling with ants. They were trying to get at our food. We put poison down and the ants disappeared. Does that make us murderers?
KERRIE	I don't know.

DANIEL	Kerrie likes cuddly bunny wabbits. Ants aren't so pwitty?
KERRIE	Shut up, Daniel.

Part Six: Purpose, Animals and People

DANIEL	I don't think things have changed much since Pasteur's time. Animals are there for humans. Pets are there to keep us company. Sheep are raised to give us food and wool. That's their purpose in life.
KERRIE	What do you mean by purpose?
DANIEL	I suppose a purpose is how something is used.
LAURA	And do people have a purpose, or only animals?
JOHN	I think we do, but we don't know what it is.
DANIEL	Isn't our purpose what we do, like my dad's a mechanic and my mom works in the supermarket? My aunt looks after her kids. Giving wool and being eaten is what sheep do.
KERRIE	My dad's unemployed. What's his purpose then?
JOHN	I'm not sure we can say we have a purpose, and if we do, it's got to be more than just what we get paid for. My dad is always saying he hates his job, but he's a good dad; he makes me laugh.
LAURA	I agree. Your dad's purpose isn't just what use he is to his boss. If we only think of what use people are to us, we aren't treating them like human beings. In the old days some farmers owned slaves and treated them like animals. They tried not to think about them as people because they only wanted to use them without it troubling their consciences.
KERRIE	Maybe we should think of animals more like people then, if we want them to be treated better. We already give them names. Maybe we should give them rights too. My purpose is whatever I set my mind on. Animals should have a right to decide on their own purpose.
DANIEL	Have you thought how many chickens supermarkets throw away because they are past their sell-by date? Those chickens' lives are wasted.
KERRIE	Only if their purpose is to feed us. They might prefer to walk the earth pecking and clucking.
DANIEL	But animals and people are different. Animals can't think or make choices like we can. It's natural that we use animals, just like animals use plants and plants use the soil. Anyway, it says in the Bible that God gave man dominion over nature.
KERRIE	Okay, so we've got power, but do we use it well?

DANIEL   I think it's okay to use animals if it's for a good purpose.

JOHN   Kerrie, you keep saying "we" have power. I don't think I have much power. Maybe scientists have power, farmers have power, teachers have power. But I don't—do I? Only adults have power.

LAURA   We have the power to try to think for ourselves. That's a good start.

REPERTOIRE AND JUDGMENT NOTES

Chapter 1: Why Dialogue?

REPERTOIRE AND JUDGMENT NOTES

Chapter 2: Dialogue Essentials

REPERTOIRE AND JUDGMENT NOTES

Chapter 3: Dialogue to Engage Students

Challenging LEARNING

REPERTOIRE AND JUDGMENT NOTES

Chapter 4: One Way to Learn *How* to Think: Develop Reasoning

REPERTOIRE AND JUDGMENT NOTES

Chapter 5: Dialogue Groupings

Challenging LEARNING

REPERTOIRE AND JUDGMENT NOTES

Chapter 6: Dialogue Detectives

Chapter 7: Dialogue Structures

REPERTOIRE AND JUDGMENT NOTES

Chapter 8: Mysteries

REPERTOIRE AND JUDGMENT NOTES

Chapter 9: Odd One Out

Challenging LEARNING

REPERTOIRE AND JUDGMENT NOTES

Chapter 10: Fortune Lines

REPERTOIRE AND JUDGMENT NOTES

Chapter 11: Philosophy for Children (P4C)

REPERTOIRE AND JUDGMENT NOTES

Chapter 12: Dialogue Exercises in P4C

REFERENCES

Adler, M. J. (1998). *The Paideia proposal.* New York, NY: Touchstone.

Alexander, R. (2006). *Towards dialogic teaching: Rethinking classroom talk* (3rd ed.). Cambridge, UK: Dialogos.

Bryk, A., & Schneider, B. (2002). *Trust in schools: A core resource for improvement.* New York, NY: Russell Sage Foundation.

Bullen, K., & Moore, K. (1999). *The influence of pupil-generated ground rules on collaborative learning in the classroom: A pilot study.* Swansea: University of Wales, Department of Psychology.

Copeland, M. (2005). *Socratic circles: Fostering critical and creative thinking in middle and high school.* Portland, ME: Stenhouse.

Dalai Lama. (1997). The statement of His Holiness the Dalai Lama. Retrieved from http://www.friendsoftibet.org/databank/hhdlgeneral/hhdlg6.html

Dewey, J. (2011). *Democracy and education.* Simon & Brown. (Original work published 1916)

Dewey, J. (1916). *Democracy and education: An introduction to the philosophy of education.* New York, NY: The Macmillan Company.

Dillon, J. T. (1994). *Using discussion in classrooms.* Buckingham, UK: Open University Press.

Drucker, P. (2007). *The effective executive* (2nd rev. ed.). Burlington, MA: Elsevier.

Friere, P. (2001). *The pedagogy of the oppressed* (30th ed.). New York, NY: Continuum International.

Hattie, J. (2009). *Visible learning: A synthesis of over 800 meta-analyses relating to achievement.* New York: Routledge.

Hattie, J. (2011). *Visible learning for teachers.* Abingdon, UK: Continuum.

Hume, D. (1739). *A treatise of human nature.* Retrieved from http://www.davidhume.org/texts/thn.html

Humphrys, J. (2004, August 26). Today programme. *BBC Radio 4.*

Kagan, S. (2013). *Kagan cooperative learning structures.* San Clemente, CA: Kagan.

Krishnamurti, J. (1989). *Think on these things.* New York, NY: HarperPerennial.

Leat, D. (2002, Summer). Mysteries. *Teaching Thinking, 8,* 42–47.

Lipman, M. (1991). *Thinking in education.* Cambridge, UK: Cambridge University Press.

Martin, S. (2011). *Using SOLO as a framework for teaching.* Invercargill, New Zealand: Essential Resources Educational.

Marzano, R. (2001). *Classroom instruction that works: Research-based strategies for increasing student achievement.* Alexandria, VA: Association for Supervision and Curriculum Development.

Marzano, R. J., Pickering, D. J., & Pollock, J. E. (2001). *Classroom instruction that works: Research-based strategies for increasing student achievement.* Alexandria, VA: Association for Supervision and Curriculum Development.

Mercer, N. (2000a). *The guided construction of knowledge.* Clevedon, UK: Multilingual Matters.

Mercer, N. (2000b). *Words and minds: How we use language to think together.* New York, NY: Routledge.

Moffett, J., & Wagner, B. (1976). *Student-centered language arts and reading, K–13* (2nd ed.). Boston, MA: Houghton Mifflin.

Nottingham. J. A. (2013). *Encouraging learning.* Abingdon, UK: Routledge.

Nottingham. J. A. (2016). *Challenging learning* (2nd ed.). Abingdon, UK: Routledge.

Nottingham, J. A. (2017). *The learning challenge: How to guide your students through the learning pit.* Thousand Oaks, CA: Corwin.

Nottingham, J. A., & Larsson, B. (2017). *Challenging learning through mindset.* Thousand Oaks, CA: Corwin.

Nottingham, J. A., & Nottingham, J. (2017). *Challenging learning through feedback: How to get the type, tone and quality of feedback right every time.* Thousand Oaks, CA: Corwin.

Nottingham, J. A., & Renton, T. M. (in press). *Challenging learning through questioning.* Thousand Oaks, CA: Corwin.

Nuthall, G. (2007). *The hidden lives of learners.* Wellington, New Zealand: NZCER Press.

Nystrand, M. (1996). *Opening dialogue: Understanding the dynamics of language and learning in the English classroom.* New York, NY: Teachers College Press.

O'Connor, C., & Michaels, S. (2007). When is dialogue "dialogic"? *Human Development, 50,* 275–285.

Resnick, L. B., Michaels, S., & O'Connor, M. C. (2010). How (well-structured) talk builds the mind. In R. J. Sternberg & D. D. Preiss (Eds.), *Innovations in educational psychology: Perspectives on learning, teaching, and human development* (pp. 163–194). New York, NY: Springer.

Richards, I. A. (1955). *Speculative instruments.* Chicago, IL: University of Chicago Press.

Rowe, M. B. (1986). Wait time: Slowing down may be a way of speeding up! *Journal of Teacher Education, 37*(1), 43–50.

Stahl, R. J. (1990). Using "think-time" behaviors to promote students' information processing, learning, and on-task participation: An instructional module. Tempe, AZ: Arizona State University.

Taylor, C. (1994). *Multiculturalism: Examining the politics of recognition.* Princeton, NJ: Princeton University Press.

Tough, J. (1977). *Talking and learning.* London, UK: Ward Lock.

Vygotsky, L. S. (1978). *Mind and society: The development of higher mental processes.* Cambridge, MA: Harvard University Press.

Wang, T.-P. (2009). Applying Slavin's cooperative learning techniques to a college EFL conversation class. *Journal of Human Resource and Adult Learning, 5*(1), 112–120.

Wegerif, R. (2002). Group intelligence. *Teaching Thinking, 3*(3), 24–27. Retrieved from http://elac.ex.ac.uk/dialogiceducation/userfiles/GrpIntelligence.pdf

Wegerif, R., & Scrimshaw, P. (1997). *Computers and talk in the primary classroom.* Clevedon, UK: Multilingual Matters.

Wilson, W. (2014). *The new freedom.* Create Space Independent Publishing Platform.

INDEX

CORWIN HAS ONE MISSION: to enhance education through intentional professional learning.

We build long-term relationships with our authors, educators, clients, and associations who partner with us to develop and continuously improve the best evidence-based practices that establish and support lifelong learning.

Solutions you want. Experts you trust. Results you need.